Hamilton Wilcox Pierson

In the Brush

Pr, Old-time Social, Political, and Religious Life in the Southwest

Hamilton Wilcox Pierson

In the Brush
Pr, Old-time Social, Political, and Religious Life in the Southwest

ISBN/EAN: 9783337132736

Printed in Europe, USA, Canada, Australia, Japan

Cover: Foto ©Suzi / pixelio.de

More available books at **www.hansebooks.com**

"Can I get to stay with you to-night, madam."

IN THE BRUSH;

OR,

OLD-TIME SOCIAL, POLITICAL, AND RELIGIOUS LIFE IN THE SOUTHWEST.

BY

REV. HAMILTON W. PIERSON, D. D.,

EX-PRESIDENT OF CUMBERLAND COLLEGE, KENTUCKY; AUTHOR OF "JEFFERSON AT MONTICELLO"; CORRESPONDING MEMBER OF THE NEW YORK HISTORICAL SOCIETY, ETC.

WITH ILLUSTRATIONS BY W. L. SHEPPARD.

NEW YORK:

D. APPLETON AND COMPANY,

1, 3, AND 5 BOND STREET.

1881.

CONTENTS.

IN THE BRUSH.

CHAPTER I.

WHY I RELATE MY EXPERIENCES IN THE SOUTHWEST.—INTRODUCTORY.

On a visit to New York, many years ago, after the first few months of my ministerial labors in the wilds of the Southwest, I met a warm personal friend, a genial, generous, noble Christian woman, who at once said to me:

"And so you are a Western missionary. Well, do tell me if anything *strange* or *funny* ever *did* happen to a missionary. Mother has taken the home-missionary papers ever since I was a child, and I always read them; and I often wonder if anything *strange* or *funny* did *ever* happen to a Western missionary."

I had recently spent three happy years in the Union Theological Seminary in that city, and had come back to attend the heart-stirring anniversaries, held in those days in the old Broadway Tabernacle, and to meet again the many friends who had followed me in my labors with their kind wishes and their prayers. Though nearly thirty years have passed since I received that greeting, I have never forgotten, and have very often recalled it. And I have as often thought that it was most natural that the churches and people at large who send forth and sustain the heroic laborers who are toiling in the varied departments of Christian effort in our newer States and Territories, should desire a much fuller account of their daily lives and labors. As many of them travel extensively, and see pioneer border-life in all its aspects and phases, I have thought it most natural and reasonable that the people should desire to know more of their adventures; more of their contact with the rough, whole-souled people with whom they so often meet and mingle; more of that strange compound of energy, recklessness, and daring, the hardy hosts who erect their log-cabins and fell the forests in the van of our American civilization, in its triumphant westward march. Only one day in seven is set apart as sacred time, and only a few hours of that day are devoted to what are generally regarded as spiritual duties. A description of these duties alone, whether performed on Sabbath-days or week-days, is a very inadequate description of missionary life as a whole. In order to perform these duties, a man must eat and drink, take care of his body, mingle with the world, and meet all his responsibilities as a man and a citizen.

In the pages that follow it will be my purpose to present a portraiture of ministerial life in the wilds of the Southwest, in all its aspects and phases, exactly as I found it. I shall attempt to portray week-day life as well as Sunday life. I shall describe scenes of wonderful and thrilling religious interest, and the most common and homely incidents of every-day life, and, as far as possible, give an idea of my life as a whole. I shall attempt to describe the politicians, preachers, and people; the country in which they live, their manners and customs, their barbecues, basket-meetings, and weddings, and all the peculiarities of their open, free, and genial *home-life* in its social, political, and religious aspects and relations. In this I shall be successful only so far as I succeed in perfectly describing their life and my own during the many years that I mingled with them.

My lady friend and questioner, to whom I have referred, was slightly mistaken in calling me a "missionary." I was not one in name. At the time of my graduation from the Theological Seminary, I was under appointment as a missionary of the American Board of Commissioners for Foreign Missions to West Africa; but hæmorrhages from my lungs prevented my entrance upon that work.

After extended travels by sea and land for nearly five years, I had so far recovered my voice as to be able to preach, and was very anxious to be about my chosen life-work. But my physicians—Dr. Gurdon Buck, Dr. Alfred C. Post, and Dr. John H. Swett, of the University Medical College—as kind as they were distinguished and skillful, told me that I would never be able to perform the duties of a settled pastor; that the study, labor, and care of such a life would completely break down my health in a very few months. They told me that I must engage in some labor that would give me a large amount of exercise in the open air; and that if it involved horseback-riding it would be all the better for my health, and probably give me more years in which to labor. I accordingly accepted an agency from the American Bible Society, which involved the exploration on horseback of the wild regions in the Southwest described in this volume. In addition to very extended travels by steamboat up and down many of the larger and smaller Southwestern and Southern rivers, I have ridden a great many thousand miles on horseback—I have no means of telling how many. For a long time I rode my horse several thousands of miles yearly. Bishop Kavenaugh, of the Methodist Episcopal Church, South, in introducing me, as an agent of the American Bible Society, to a Southwestern conference over which he was presiding, told them that, "although a Presbyterian," I had "out-itinerated the Itineracy itself."

I spent a night with the Governor of a South-western State, at the house of his sister, who was the wife of an Episcopal clergyman. We lodged in the same room, occupying separate beds, as was very common in that region. The Governor was genial and social, and we conversed until long after midnight. We talked of the hills, valleys, and mountains, of families and communities, of the customs, manners, and peculiarities of different classes of people, over a very wide portion of the State. As I was about to leave in the morning, the Governor said to me:

"Sir, you know *more about this State*, and *more people in it*, than any man I ever saw."

I replied: "I am surprised, Governor, to hear you make that statement. I know that politicians canvass the State most thoroughly; that you are expected to make speeches in every county, and in as many neighborhoods as possible; and that you try to shake hands with as many as you can of those that you expect and wish to vote for you. As you were born and educated in the State, and have canvassed it so thoroughly and successfully, I supposed that you knew a great deal more about it, and a great many more people in it, than I do."

"I do not," he replied, very positively, "and I never saw a man in my life who did."

I state these facts as my reason and justification for writing this book; that my readers may understand that I am not a novice in regard to the things whereof I write; that I know whereof I affirm. Indeed, I will tell them confidentially that I have obtained a "degree," one not so easily acquired as some others, and more honored in the wilds of the country. It is " B. B.," and means Brush-Breaker. The exposition of the full meaning of this " degree " will explain the origin and meaning of my title to this book.

In attending a conference, presbytery, association, or other ecclesiastical meeting in the wilds of the country, as the old veteran and other preachers were pointed out to me by some friend, he would say :

" That is Father A——. He is an old *Brush-Breaker*"—and all the younger men would press forward to shake his hand and do him honor; or, " That is Brother B——. He has broken a right smart chance of brush"; or, " That is young Brother C——, wonderfully self-satisfied and conceited, as you see. The sisters have flattered him so much that he has got the '*big head*' badly. He will be sent to Brush College, to break brush a year or two, and will come back humbled, and will make a laborious and useful man"; or, " That is our devoted and beloved young Brother D——. His soul is all on fire with love for his Master, and he will thank God for the privilege of going anywhere in the Brush to preach and sing of Jesus and his salvation."

This use of the word *Brush* enters largely into the figures of speech of the people of the Southwest. On one occasion I heard a Methodist bishop preach on a Sabbath morning to a very large congregation, composed of the Conference, the people of the village, and the visitors in attendance. During the first half of his sermon, which was extemporaneous, he did not preach with his accustomed clearness and power. His thoughts were evidently very much confused, and it was rather painful than otherwise to witness his struggle to get the mastery of his mind and subject. But he accomplished this at length, and closed his sermon with great power and effect. In returning from church, a young circuit-rider said to me:

"Didn't you think the Bishop got badly *brushed* in the first part of his sermon? I sometimes get so brushed in my sermons that I think I will never try to preach again. It's a comfort to a beginner to know that an old preacher sometimes gets brushed."

Figurative language of this kind abounded among the people of the Southwest, and was very expressive. These provincialisms had usually grown out of the peculiar life and habits of the people. Many of them seem to have originated in the perils of early flat-boat navigation—when they were accustomed to float down-stream by daylight, and tie up to some stump or tree for the night! Woe betide the cargo, boat, and crew, if that to which they had "made fast" failed them in the darkness of the night! Hence, as I suppose, this provincialism.

If I made inquiries in regard to the character of a

man who had been recommended to me for a Bible distributor, I was not told that he was a reliable or an unreliable man, but, "He'll do to tie to," or "He won't do to tie to"; and if the case was particularly bad, "He won't do to tie to in a calm, let alone a storm." As there were so many perils in this kind of navigation, those were regarded as extremely fortunate who reached their destination in safety, and could send back word that they had made the trip; hence, "to make the trip" was a universal synonym for success. And so, when a novice attempted to make a speech, preach a sermon, address a jury, or engage in any kind of business, the people predicted his success or failure by saying, "He'll make the trip," or "He won't make the trip." They never said of a young man, or an old widower, that he was addressing or courting a lady, but, "He is setting to her," a figure of speech derived from bird-hunting with setter-dogs, as I suppose. When such a suit had been unsuccessful, they did not say the lady rejected or "mittened" her suitor, but, "She kicked him." The first time I ever heard that figure used was at a social gathering in Richmond, Virginia, in 1843, where the belle of the evening was a Miss Burfoot. After being introduced to her by a friend, he told me confidentially that she had recently "kicked" Mr. H——, a gentleman present, to whom he had already introduced me. To be "kicked" by a Bur-foot seemed to me a more than usually striking figure.

When many persons were striving for the same object, or where there were rival aspirants for the heart and hand of the same lady, they said of the successful one, " The tallest pole takes the persimmon."

I was once present at an ecclesiastical meeting in the Brush, where motions of different kinds were piled upon each other, until the greatest confusion prevailed as to the state of the question before the body, and the moderator was appealed to to give his decision in the matter. I did not fully comprehend his decision, but it was clear and satisfactory to the body over which he was presiding, all of whom, like himself, were old and experienced hunters. Arising to his feet, as became a presiding officer thus appealed to, and lifting his tall, lank form until his head was among the rafters of the low log schoolhouse, he hesitated a moment, and then said, " Brethren, my decision is that you are all ahead of the hounds."

These are but specimens of the figurative language —the provincialisms—that abound among the people of the Southwest.

I do not, therefore, in the pages that follow, speak of my travels in the " wilderness " or " forests " or " hills " or " mountains " of the Southwest, but adopt a more comprehensive term, universally prevalent in the regions explored, and describe some of my experiences in the Brush.

Though I commenced my labors in the South as

a general agent and superintendent of the colporteur operations of the American Tract Society in 1843 —ten years before my first visit to the Southwest—though I became acquainted with its *home-life*, as that life could only be learned, by such extended horseback travels, and such religious labors, prosecuted with all the energy and all the enthusiasm of early vigorous manhood, I shall devote this volume to descriptions of *home-life* in the Southwest. My reasons for this will be obvious and approved at a glance. Very little that would be new can now be written of the old-time home-life in the South. The fascinating and beautiful descriptions of Southern social life given us in the letters of Hon. William Wirt, the distinguished Attorney-General of the United States, in his "British Spy"; the full and minute biographies of Washington, Jefferson, Patrick Henry, and others, so exhaustive of every feature of this life; with the matchless descriptions of the inimitable Thackeray, and other later writers, leave very little to be said in illustration of this theme. But the true, the real old-time social, political, and religious home-life of the people of the Southwest is almost unknown to the great mass of the American people. Comparatively little has been written which is the result of extended personal contact with, and intimate personal knowledge of, the people. They have been largely the subjects of exaggeration and caricature.

In this field I have garnered many rich and golden

sheaves, where no other reaper had ever thrust in the sickle.   Here I have drawn word-pictures of many scenes in the social life of a generation, and a state of civilization, rapidly passing away, never to reappear, that otherwise would have had no memorial only as perpetuated in the traditions of the people.   I will only add that I am indebted to no library, to no book, not even to a newspaper, for a single fact presented in this volume.   They were all gathered incidentally while laboriously engaged in the duties of my profession, as a general agent of the American Bible Society, and while traveling for years in the interests of the college over which I was called to preside.   They all relate to the *ante-bellum* period in the history of our country.

CHAPTER II.

HAVING received my commission as an agent for the American Bible Society, and completed my preparations for entering upon my work as far as I could do so in New York, I left that city for one of the important cities of the Southwest, which was to be my headquarters. I knew at the outset that I could not reach the wild regions I was to explore by railroad, steamboat, stage, or even with my own private conveyance; I knew that I could climb hills and mountains, follow blind bridle-paths, ford rivers and swollen streams, only on horseback. I had several years before had some two years' experience in constant horseback travel in labors similar to those I was now entering upon, as superintendent of the colporteur operations of the American Tract Society in Virginia. There I had floundered in the marshes and swamps of "Tidewater," and been lost amid the rugged rocks and dense forests high up the sides and in the loftiest summits of the Blue Ridge and other mountains. I knew that I must have a horse. This was indispensable. More than that, I wanted a good horse, a horse broken expressly for the saddle. To be churned for years—bump, bump, bump—upon a hard-trotting horse, that was out of the question with me. I had but a small stock of health and physical strength at best, and none to spare in that way. My old friend Rev. Dr. Sprole, then of Washington, D. C., afterward of West Point, New York, and now of Detroit, Michigan, used to tell me, in Washington, that "Brother Leete," one of my co-workers in the circulation of the publications of the American Tract Society, "was one of the most self-denying Christians he had ever seen—in that he had patience to drive such a miserable old horse in transporting his books over the hills and mountains of Pennsylvania," where he had known him. But I was not anxious to illustrate that particular type of piety. I did not care to let my "light *so* shine." I wanted not only a good saddle-horse, but a faithful, reliable animal. I wanted one that I could hitch to the limb of a tree, in the midst of scores or hundreds of other horses, and leave there without any concern, while I preached in a log meeting-house, or at a "stand" erected in a grove at some cross-roads, or at a camp-meeting, or wherever else I should be able to meet and address the people. I wanted a hardy horse, that could live on the coarsest food, and stand during the coldest nights in log stables that afforded but a little more protection from the wind and cold than a rail fence. I wanted an easy-going, fleet horse, that would take me, without great personal fatigue or needless waste of time, over a wide extent of country. I wanted a horse that would scare at nothing—that, as I had opportunity, I could lead up a plank or two, on board a noisy stern-wheel or other Western steamer, along the banks of the rivers, across wharf-boats, or wherever I might wish to embark for a hundred miles or more to save a few days of horse-back travel.

The "qualities" that I looked for in a horse were numerous and rare. I was so fortunate as to find one that possessed all that I have enumerated and many more. Was I not fortunate? Was I wrong in regarding my good fortune as a special providence? But I did not easily find this treasure. It was after a long search and many failures. Unable to find such a horse as I was willing to purchase at once, I determined to enter upon my work and get along for a time as best I could.

I therefore took stage for a point about fifty miles from headquarters, where, after a conference with the officers of the County Bible Society, I procured a horse for several days in order to plunge into the Brush, make a circuit of the county, and preach at a number of places in accordance with a programme that their familiarity with the country enabled them to make out for me. They arranged to send my appointments ahead to all these points but one, where I was to preach the next day, which was the Sabbath.

I will here state that the great object of my mission to the Brush was to effect a thorough exploration of the field assigned to me, and, either by sale or gift, supply every family with a copy of the Bible, except such as positively declined to receive it. To accomplish this, I wished to gain personal knowledge of each county, to preach at as many points as possible, in order to give information in regard to the character and operations of the American Bible Society and the work to be done, collect as much money as possible to meet the expenses of this work, find and employ suitable men to canvass the counties and visit without fail every family, and then order a supply of Bibles and Testaments from the Society's house in New York, give them their instructions, and set them at work. Such was my mission.

Saturday, after dinner, I mounted my horse for a ride of thirteen miles to a small county-seat village where I was to spend the Sabbath. The country was rough and broken, with light, sandy soil, sparsely covered with small, scrubby oak-trees, called " black-jacks," and the region of country was known as the " Barrens." It was barren enough. The houses were mostly poor and comfortless, the barns small log structures, with no stables, sheds, or covering of any kind for the cattle. They were poor and scrawny, and their backs described a section of a semicircle as they drew themselves into as much of a heap as possible—their only protection against the bleak February winds. The swine were of the original "root-hog-or-die" variety, their long, well-developed snouts being their most prominent feature. Occasionally black, dirty, ragged slaves—"uncles," "aunties," and their children—revealed the whites of their eyes and their shining ivory as they stared earnestly at the rare sight of a passing stranger. No one, with the kindest heart and the most amiable disposition, would be able to pronounce the country attractive or the ride a pleasant one. On arriving at the village, I rode to a very plain house to which I had been directed, and received a most warm and cordial welcome. Large pine-knots were soon blazing and roaring in the ample fireplace to relieve me of the most wretchedly disagreeable of all sensations of cold—those of a damp, clammy, chilly winter day in the Southwest. As soon as it could possibly be prepared, I was seated with the family at a bountiful supper. The aroma of the richest coffee was afloat in the air, and the rarest of fried chicken and hot corn-bread were smoking before me, flanked with a superabundance of other dishes, that showed the perfect country housekeeper.

My host and hostess were Presbyterians, and this was the reception they gladly gave to any minister

who visited them in their seclusion, and preached for
their little church. The bell was rung, and I preached
that (Saturday) night to a very small audience who assembled at this brief notice. The church stood within
a very few rods of the spot where Abraham Lincoln
was born.

On Sabbath morning a somewhat larger congregation assembled from the village and country around,
including some from the homes I had passed the day
before, and I made a full exposition of the character
and operations of the American Bible Society, explained the work about to be undertaken in their own
county, and made as urgent and eloquent an appeal
as I was able to, for funds to supply their own poor
with the Bible, and meet the expenses of this benevolent and Christian work. To adopt the language universal in all this region, they "lifted a collection" for
me which amounted to six dollars and eighty-five cents.
At 3 P. M. I heard a sermon preached by the clergyman,
my kind friend and host at the other county-seat,
who, according to arrangement, came over to spend
the Sabbath with me, and fill a regular appointment.
At night I preached for them again. Altogether it
was to me a very pleasant day.

Monday morning I rode back to the county-seat.
There was a hard rain-storm, and I got very wet.
Tuesday morning I started on a preaching tour of
several days, to fulfill the appointments that had been

made for me. I traveled several miles to see an old
man who had been recommended for a colporteur to
canvass the county; was pleased with him, and he
was afterward employed. After dinner he piloted me
through rough, broken barrens, such as I have already
described, to the place where I was to preach that
night. We reached there, but my "appointment" had
not. I did not wonder it had lost its way. I lost
mine a good many times that week. However, we
learned that the next day was the regular appointment
for the Methodist preacher who rode that circuit, and
I would then have an opportunity to address the people. We spent the night very comfortably with
Brother H——, to whom I had been directed, who
belonged to the class of farmers or planters known
among these people as "not rich, but good livers."
In other portions of the country he would have been
spoken of as a man "in comfortable circumstances."
Wednesday morning we rode to a small Methodist
chapel bearing the name of my host. His house had
for years been the home where laborious and self-
denying itinerant preachers, often hungry, wet, and
weary, had found most welcome and needed refreshment and rest. A kind Providence has dotted the
wilds of the country with many such hospitable homes
—I have often found them and enjoyed their cheer—
whose owners, more rich in generous, noble impulses
than in worldly goods, have thus laid up treasures in

heaven, the exceeding riches and abundance of which they will only fully comprehend and enjoy when they hear the approving—"Inasmuch as ye have done it unto one of the least of these my brethren, ye have done it unto me." On arriving at the chapel, which was a small, unplastered frame building, I was introduced by my host to Brother M——, the "preacher in charge," and received from him an old itinerant's cordial shake of the hand and welcome to his circuit. After a few moments' conversation he thrust his arm into mine, as though we had been acquainted for years, and we strolled off among the black-jacks to await the arrival of the congregation.

"What church do you belong to, Brother P——?" said he.

"I am a Presbyterian, sir," I responded.

"I am glad to hear it, glad to hear it," said he. "Brother Y——, the last agent of the Bible Society, was a Methodist, and we've had Methodist agents a good while. I am glad there is a change. I heard there would be, at Conference. All our brethren will be glad to see and welcome you."

As Brother M—— was the first real itinerant that I met on his circuit deep in the Brush, I will present him a little more fully to my readers. He wore on his head, drawn well down over his ears and eyes, a cheap cloth cap, badly soiled and faded. I do not now recall the color of his coat. I remember that it was of

coarse material and ragged, with a particularly large
rent under one of the armholes. His pantaloons were
genuine butternut-colored jeans. I have no doubt that
the cloth was the gift of some good sister, woven in
her own loom, and all that she was able to give in
making up his scanty salary. The most of the audience, both men and women, were clothed in the same
home-made material. For myself, I was dressed in
all respects as I had been the last time I had preached
in New York. I did not like the contrast between
myself and the congregation; and on my return to the
city I laid aside my entire black suit, and procured
a second-hand snuff-colored overcoat, costing eight dollars, jean pantaloons, and a soft hat, in which I felt
much more at ease on my next return to the Brush.
To anticipate a little, I will say that in my desire to
carry out the Pauline example in becoming all things
to all men, I went a little too far; for I wore my
Brush suit to Conference, where I met this same
preacher, and scores of his brethren with whom I
had become acquainted, dressed in black, and presenting a contrast quite to my disadvantage. I had, however, gone there on horseback, traveling and preaching
through the wildest brush country, with only such
changes of clothing as I could carry in my saddle-
bags. If I was a little mortified at my personal appearance when the presiding elder introduced me to the
venerable bishop, and he introduced me to the Conn

ference, and they all arose to their feet to do me honor, and welcome me as the representative of the American Bible Society, I had at least this satisfaction, that with the large audience present my dress would do something to correct the popular impression, very widely prevalent in the Brush, that " Presbyterian ministers preach for good clothes."

One by one the small congregation arrived at the chapel — men, women, and children — on horseback. When they had all assembled, we went in, and I preached, and they "lifted a collection" amounting to three dollars and twenty-five cents. After dining with Brother M——, at a house near by, I mounted my horse for a long ride, to reach my appointment for the night. My kind friends gave me a great many directions, and I started out. There was nothing worthy of the name of a public road. There were wagon-tracks and paths running in all directions among the black-jacks, and crossing each other at all angles. Whenever, for a short distance, there was a fence on both sides of a road, *that* was called a "lane." One track would lead me to the back side of a tobacco-patch, where it ended ; another led me where some rails had been " mauled " and recently hauled away. The roads leading to plantations were more worn, and looked more like the " main traveled road," than those that were intended for public highways. I inquired my way at each plantation that I passed, and every

2

other opportunity; and these were far too rare for my
wants. Once I saw, from an elevation, a peach-tree
in bloom in the distance. It was like the human foot-
print in the sand to Robinson Crusoe on his lonely
island. I said, "There is a sign of humanity," and started for it. But when I reached it the log-cabin near
which it was planted was empty, and I started out
again into the labyrinths of paths. Often that afternoon, and oftener in the years that followed, when I
have been lost in the Brush, I exclaimed, "Blessed be
the man that devised our national system of 'sectional
surveys'!" I do not know what man or men devised
it, but I do know that the country owes him or them
a debt of gratitude it can never pay. Where section-
lines are established, there roads are located, roads running at right angles, and school-districts, townships,
and larger communities have definite boundaries; and
every neighborhood and farm may have the benefit of
established and good roads. These barrens, like vast
regions of country over which I have traveled, never
had the benefit of such a survey. The original settlers
had found places where the land, timber, water, etc.,
suited them, and had measured off, perhaps with a
pole or grape-vine, hundreds or thousands of acres in
any shape their fancy directed—their surveys often
overlapping each other at various points. Hence in-
terminable lawsuits in regard to boundaries, and the
greater calamity of having no established lines for a

uniform system of roads. A learned author has said, "You may judge the civilization of a country by its roads." If this is a true criterion, there is a vast extent of country over which I have traveled, in the Southwest and South, that will take a very low rank in the scale of civilization. I remember one man in the Brush who told me he had raised that year three hogsheads of tobacco, but the roads were so bad that the transportation of his crop, sixty miles to market, had cost him one hogshead of tobacco—one third of the proceeds of his summer's work! One of the most prominent causes of the development and growth of our Western States is the manner in which they were surveyed, and their system of roads; one of the greatest hindrances to the prosperity of other and large sections of our country is that they have had no such survey, and are not likely to have any such roads.

I reached the house of Mr. R——, to whom I was directed, soon after sundown, and learned that my appointment had reached him, and he was expecting me. He at once gave orders to his boys to get the shell-bark-hickory torches that they had provided to light us home, and without dismounting he led my way, on foot, about a mile, to an unpainted, unplastered, barn-like-looking building, known as "Blue Knobs Church." A few tallow-candles shed their glimmering rays upon the upturned faces of the not large audience that listened to my description of the Bible House, its numerous presses, and vast facilities for publishing the Bible; and, in response to my appeal for funds for the noble cause I represented, they "lifted a collection" amounting to ninety-four cents. In the light of the torches thoughtfully provided for me, I climbed up the sides of the knob—the higher elevations of land in this region are called "knobs"—to the home of my host. Supper was now prepared for the family and myself; and I learned that it was the custom of the people to defer supper until this hour, whenever they had meetings at night.

Fairly seated in the house, I saw such a group of little children as I had never seen before, belonging to one family. We had not talked long before the father volunteered an explanation. He told me his wife had died, leaving nine children, one but a few days old. Not many months after, he had married a young widow with three children, as young as his three youngest, and one had been born since their marriage. Of the thirteen present, the majority were under five years old. Subsequently, in my travels, I spent a night with a family where there was a large number of young children, and I asked the mother the age of the eldest and the youngest. The eldest would be six years old the next June; the youngest was six weeks old. She had six healthy children, that had been born in less than six years, and none of them were twins.

On Thursday I started early in the morning and

rode through a country that differed but little from that through which I had passed the day before, to the place of my appointment. On going to the hall of the secret society, where I was to preach, I learned that it was the night of their regular weekly meeting, and they could not yield their room to me. Such collisions are not unfrequent in the Brush, and the people describe them by a very striking figure of speech, which gives some idea of their sports and tastes. They say of them that " the appointments locked horns." I did not care to test the strength of my neck, and therefore, as was altogether proper in the circumstances, did not preach. That night I slept in the loft of a log-cabin. It was entirely unceiled, and the roof was so low that I had to stoop to make my way to my bed; and when in it I could easily place my hands upon the roof-boards and rafters. The openings between the logs afforded abundant ventilation. In the morning, I found such conveniences as were afforded for washing, not in my room, but out-of-doors, at the side of the well. Afterward, I slept in hundreds of such cabin-lofts—slept in them until the sight of smoky, dingy roof-boards and rafters was wellnigh as familiar a sight on opening my eyes in the morning, as the sky overhead when I went to the well to wash, sometimes in a basin or dish, but often by having the water poured upon my hands from a gourd. I remember one occasion when, after traveling for weeks in the Brush, I arrived at a small county-seat village, and spent the night in a new building that had recently been erected for a young ladies' seminary. In the morning, as I opened my eyes, they were greeted with the sight of new white-plastered walls above and around me. The sight was so rare that it thrilled me with joy. The smooth, clean plaster seemed absolutely beautiful. I have never since experienced more delightful sensations in gazing upon the most magnificent paintings. I can see now the new, cheap bedstead, the clean sheets, the blue-calico window-curtains, the white walls, and recall the sensations of intense pleasure that they inspired. It was as if I had slept for weeks in a dungeon, and awoke in the most delightful home.

On Friday morning I started early again, and by a most difficult and crooked route through the "barrens," made my way to the residence of "Uncle Billy II——," to whose hospitality I had been commended. Here I found a brick house on a turnpike-road, and "Uncle Billy" was a "good liver." He went with me at night to a small church, located upon a stream, near a grist-mill, and I preached, and "lifted a collection" amounting to four dollars and five cents.

On Saturday morning, my appointments for the week being all fulfilled, I took the turnpike and started for the county-seat. I was never so grateful for a good road, and never so willing and glad to pay toll.

At various points along the "pike," as it was universally called, I saw tracks leading off into the woods, and was told that they were known as "shunpikes," and that some people in traveling would take these and go through the woods around the toll-gates, in order to avoid paying toll. I had not the slightest disposition to perpetrate that immorality and meanness. I stuck to the pike as one would to an old friend and guide, after having been bewildered and lost in the most perilous ways. It was comfortable not to be asking and getting "directions" that were a good deal more incomprehensible and past finding out than the blind roads and paths I was trying to follow. I was most happy to be freed from the disagreeable feelings of uncertainty and anxiety as to whether or not I was in the right road or path, and was making progress in the right direction, or I should be obliged to retrace my steps. As I rode on thus, dark clouds rolled up the sky and it began to rain. I unstrapped my umbrella from my saddle, and, as I spread it, my horse, that had seemed as gentle as any horse could be, shot from under me with a movement so sudden and swift, that I struck but once on his rump, rolled off behind him, and he went tearing into the woods at the side of the "pike." I never could understand how my feet were disentangled from the stirrups, and how I fell upon the hard turnpike-road without being hurt at all. But I know that that kind

Protector was with me who has preserved me through so many years of travel upon oceans, lakes, rivers, and during unnumbered thousands of miles of travel by railroad, stage, and on horseback, over the roughest and wildest portions of the land, without ever suffering a more serious accident than this. I followed my horse into the woods, but could not find him, and walked about four miles to the village in the rain.

After dinner, my kind clerical friend and host rode with me several miles to find my horse, and my saddle-bags that he had carried into the woods with him, but our search was in vain. At night, after our return, a black boy—a slave—who had found my horse in the woods, brought him to me, and received his reward. The saddle-bags I never found. More than all else I regretted the loss of my small Bible, that had been my constant companion during all my school-days, and in all my travels by sea and by land for many years before.

Sunday was a cold, rainy, cheerless day. I preached to a very small congregation that assembled in the morning, and "lifted a collection" amounting to nine dollars and five cents. In the afternoon and at night it rained so hard that there were no public services.

Monday, I spent the forenoon with the officers of the county Bible Society, instructing them in their duties and aiding them in writing their reports. In the afternoon I attended a funeral that was less like a

funeral than any I had ever witnessed, and seemed
more strange to me than anything I had yet seen.
The clergyman invited me to go with him to the graveyard, where he had engaged to be present at the burial.
The funeral party was from the country. The coffin
was conveyed in a large farm-wagon drawn by six
mules. The mud was very deep and very red. The
family and neighbors followed on horseback, a straggling company, attempting to maintain no semblance
of a procession or any kind of order. The women were
dressed as I have since seen thousands of. Brush-women
dressed. They had long riding-skirts made of coarse
cotton-factory cloth, dyed the inevitable butternut-color.
Their bonnets were of the simplest possible construction, made of any kind of calico, stiffened and bent over
the top of the head in such form as to protect the
neck, and project a long distance beyond the face, and
usually called "sun-bonnets." The company all rode
as near the grave as they conveniently could, and
with the exception of those who officiated in lowering
the coffin into the grave, they all sat upon their
horses while the clergyman performed his brief religious services. There were no sable mourning-weeds.
The contrast in colors and dress from those usually
seen at a funeral, as well as in all the forms generally
observed on such an occasion, impressed me very
strangely. On another occasion I attended a funeral
where the company followed after the corpse in the

same straggling manner, though the most of them were on foot, and on their way to the graveyard they climbed the fences and went across-lots by a shorter route, leaving the hearse to go around the road, and they were at the grave to receive and bury the corpse when the hearse arrived. This was not from any want of respect, for the person buried was a college graduate and lawyer. It was simply their way of doing things.

On Tuesday, having completed all my arrangements for the exploration and supply of the county with Bibles, I took stage and returned to headquarters. As from time to time I received the reports of the Bible-distributor, and learned of the amount sold, and of the large number of families destitute who gladly received as a gift this inestimable treasure, I felt that in all my toils and personal privations in thus exploring the Brush, I had not labored in vain nor spent my strength for naught. In the great day, when all the good results of these labors shall be revealed, I know that there will be no cause for regret, but much for joy.

I was now better prepared than ever before to understand just what I needed and all that I needed to complete my outfit for the Brush. My experience in horseback-riding had been particularly instructive on this subject. After somewhat extended but fruitless search and inquiry for a horse, such as I needed in that vicinity, I took steamer for a great horse-market a hundred and fifty miles distant. Here I found great droves of horses, in vast stables, attended by scores of jockeys, all wide awake and eager to show me the very article that I wanted. I went from stable to stable, looked at a good many, heard the most satisfactory statements from their voluble owners in regard to the qualities of those that were brought out and submitted to my special inspection, mounted some of them and rode a short distance to test their qualities, but did not purchase. Indeed, I became entirely satisfied that I was not as verdant in regard to horse-flesh as from my pale looks and clerical appearance they generally took me to be. Though a clergyman, and the son of a clergyman, my father had penetrated the wilderness of Western New York, purchased a farm, and erected his log-cabin west of the Genesee River in 1807, when there was but a single log-house where Rochester now stands. Hence, from my childhood I had enjoyed the invaluable advantages of farm-life and labors. I had ridden colts, driven and worked horses, and learned what is hardly worth less in the future battle of life than all that is acquired in college and professional schools.

While looking through these large stables I heard of a horse that had been sent to a stable to be sold on account of some changes in the family of the owner. I went and looked at her, and was greatly pleased. I mounted her, rode a few miles, and returned perfectly satisfied and delighted. In a short time I paid the price asked, and was her happy owner. It was love at first sight, love that never failed, but grew stronger and stronger through all the years that we journeyed together. I took her on board the steamer with me, and returned to headquarters. Next I procured saddle, bridle, halter, spurs, leggins, and saddle-bags. For leggins I bought a yard and a half of butternut jean, which was cut into two equal parts, and the buttons and button-holes so arranged that I could wrap them tightly around my legs from a short distance above my knees, and button them on. They were secured from slipping down by a pair of strings which were wound about the legs both above and below the knees, in such a manner as not to interfere with their free movement in either riding or walking. A good deal of skill, as well as a good deal of awkwardness, may be displayed in putting on and tying on a pair of leggins; and when a man displays unusual facility and skill in this matter in his travels through the Brush, he is at once taken to be either an itinerant preacher—or a horse-thief. In long horseback journeys these leggins are invaluable as a protection against mud, rain, and cold. I have traveled over the muddiest roads, many days and weeks, when, on arriving at the house of some hospitable friend, I was so completely bespattered and covered with mud that I looked very much like the roads through which I had been traveling; but, on taking off my leggins and overcoat, I laid aside the most of the mud with them, and so presented a very respectable appearance.

But the saddle-bags were indispensable. In them I carried all the changes in my wardrobe, and all such articles for my personal comfort as one can have whose home is on horseback; together with such reports, documents, and papers, as were indispensable to me in the prosecution of my labors. With a large blanket-shawl rolled compactly together, and strapped with my umbrella behind my saddle upon a pad attached to it for this purpose, I was prepared to travel without any regard to rain or weather.

Behold me, then, with my new and complete outfit, mounted and starting for the Brush, in a broad-brimmed white hat, snuff-colored overcoat, butternut-dyed pantaloons, leggins, heavy boots, and spurs. My saddle-bags were thrown across the saddle, and my blanket-shawl and umbrella strapped behind it. As I rode out of the city into the country, I met a countryman on his way to town, who greeted me with a pleasant "How d'y, sir?" and, as he scanned with a pleasant face my outfit, he added, "Traveling, sir?" A countryman, and to the "manner born," that was his quick recognition and approval of the perfection and completeness of my outfit for the Brush. Two negroes, who were felling a huge tree in the dense forest at the roadside, paused in their labor, and manifested their approval with a broad African grin, and " Mighty nice hoss, dat, massa!"

In my next chapter I shall make good these comments.

CHAPTER III.

I THINK a good horse is worthy of a niche in the temple of fame. I know that many men have been immortalized in song and eloquence, and had magnificent monuments erected to their memory, who have never done one half as much for the good of the world as the faithful animal I rode so many years, through the wilds of the Southwest, in the service of the American Bible Society. But very few *men* have done as much to promote the circulation of the Word of God, "without note or comment," as she did in those years of faithful labor.

If there be a paradise where there are purling streams, grateful shade, and fat pastures for *horses* that have been faithful and true, I am sure that she has a high rank in "the noble army" of horses that in sunshine and in storm, with unflagging devotion, have borne itinerant pioneer preachers through mud and rain, and sleet and snow, as with glowing, burning zeal they have prosecuted their heroic Christian labors.

All honor to the itinerant's faithful horse—my own among the number! My very pen seems to catch new inspiration, and dance with delight, as I attempt her eulogy.

In fact, she shrank from no toil in the prosecution of this good work. She never kept me from fulfilling an appointment by refusing to ford a river. She never hesitated to enter any canebrake it was necessary for me to cross, and, though the canes were ever so thick and tangled, and resisted her progress like so many ropes or cords around her breast, yet she pressed carefully and firmly against them, until they yielded to her power, and we emerged safely from the thicket. She never flinched from climbing the steepest mountain-paths, where I had to hold on to her mane with both hands to keep from sliding off behind her; and then she would as kindly perform the more difficult feat of descending such paths, stepping carefully and firmly so as not to stumble or fall, while I kept my position in the saddle by holding on to the crupper with one hand and guiding her with the other. In a word, she never failed or disappointed me at any time, in any place, or in any particular.

She was of medium size, light-sorrel color, white face, and in all respects of admirable form and mold. She had been broken for the saddle to either pace, trot, or gallop, and each gait was about as easy and perfect as possible. In long journeys of weeks, and sometimes of months, her movements were always free and fleet, and by alternating from one gait to another she bore me about as easily and gently as one could well wish to be carried on horseback. But her kind, affectionate disposition was her crowning excellence. I never hitched her and went into a house for a long or short stay, that she did not greet me as soon as I opened the door on my return with her affectionate whinny. She would recognize me among the congregation, as I came out of any church where I had preached, or wherever she could see me in the largest gatherings of people, and always with the same warm salutation. Whenever I went to her stable in the morning, or wherever I approached her after a brief separation, her demonstrations of affection were as strong as they could well be without human powers.

On one occasion I rode up to the bank of a small river, very near its mouth, and hailed the ferryman on the opposite side. While waiting for him to cross, I led her down upon the planks which extended a short distance into the river, that she might drink. Wading into the water, she stepped beyond the planks and instantly sank to her breast in the mud. It was the sediment that had been deposited there by numerous freshets. As she went down the entire depth of her fore-legs in an instant, she made one desperate effort to extricate herself, but in vain. She seemed to comprehend her condition perfectly, turned to me with

a beseeching look and groan, and did not make another
struggle. I told her to lie still, and started on a run
to get some teamsters, whom I had met with their
large six-horse teams as I rode up to the river-bank,
to help me in getting her out. They kindly came to
my aid, and by putting my saddle-girth under her
breast, and tying ropes to each end of it, they lifted
her out of the mud by main strength. When she was
fairly on her feet, her demonstrations of gratitude were
most remarkable. She thanked me over and over
again as plainly and strongly as horse-language would
possibly admit of, danced around me with delight, per-
sisted in rubbing her nose against me in the most
affectionate manner, and showed a joy that seemed
wellnigh human. It was warm summer weather, and
on reaching the hotel on the opposite shore I had her
legs and her entire body from the tips of her ears to
the end of her tail thoroughly washed and rubbed
dry. After dinner I resumed my journey, and she
was as well as ever.

Everywhere, during all the years that I traveled in
the Brush, my Jenny—for that was the name I gave
her—made friends for herself and me. If I rode up
to a house upon a plantation, hailed it according to
the custom of the country, and was welcomed to its
hospitalities by the owner, he would call a negro servant:

"Ho! boy, carry this horse to the stable and take
good care of her. D'ye hear?"

When I dismounted, she understood that her long day's journey was ended, and knew where she was going as well as the servant did. When mounted, she would start with a fleet pace that was almost as gentle in its movements as the rocking of a cradle; which would make the rider roll the white of his eyes with the supremest African delight. Very often I have seen them turn their faces, beaming with satisfaction, and cast back furtive glances upon groups of young Africans that were gazing after them with an admiration that was only equaled by their envy of the rider's happy lot. Before reaching the stable a friendship, if not affection, was established that insured the most liberal allowance of "fodder" and corn, and the most thorough currying, brushing, and care. I have no doubt that on many such occasions they promised themselves a pleasant stolen night-ride, to visit friends on some near or remote plantation, and that they did not forget or fail to make good their promises. When I sometimes had occasion to protract my stay for several days, it was amusing to listen to the frequent applications from young Africa to ride her to the brook and water her. They were intensely solicitous that she should not fail to get water—or themselves rides! At all places, whether on cultivated plantations or deep in the Brush, whether she was cared for by black or white, she received the same kind attention. Hence she was always in the best order and condition

—always able and ready to take me the longest journeys, through any amount of mud and mire, and over the roughest roads, wherever it was necessary for me to go. I am sure that the people were the more glad to see me on her account. My honored instructor, the venerable President Nott, of Union College, in his lectures on the "Beautiful," used to say:

"Young gentlemen, undoubtedly the two most beautiful objects in nature are a beautiful horse and a beautiful lady. I hope you will not think me ungallant in putting the horse before the lady." I gratified the love of the beautiful in a fine horse, and so won their esteem and love. But I was often as much surprised and gratified at her behavior in her travels with me upon Western steamboats as upon land. On one occasion I took her on board a large New Orleans steamer with a deck-load of mules, horses, sheep, etc., and rode some two hundred miles. I reached the place of my destination about midnight, and was obliged to land at that hour. She was standing immediately back of the wheel-house, and on the side of the boat toward the shore. But the boat was so loaded that I was obliged to lead her a long distance around by the stern, past the heels of braying mules and bellowing cattle, to the point opposite the place from which I had started; then forward, crossing the boat immediately in front of the roaring wood-fires, which were on the same deck, and on to the bow, where I led her down the plank on to a large wharf-boat. I then led her the entire length of this boat, and down a long plank-way to the shore. And all this through the indescribable din and confusion made by mates and deck-hands in landing freight, passengers, and baggage, and the deafening screech of the whistle in blowing off steam. When I took her by the bits and said, "Come, Jenny," she placed her head against my shoulder and followed me all this long, crooked, noisy route, with the confidence of a child. I had led her on and off a great many noisy steamers, but that was the most notable instance of all.

But my Jenny had some other qualities which I should never have discovered had they not been made known to me by others. Elsewhere in this volume I have spoken at length of my visit to a celebrated watering-place, and of the numerous gamblers and other strange characters that I met there. It was in the midst of a very wild region. When I had arrived within a few hours' ride of the springs, I stopped to dine at a house of private entertainment. A large four-horse stage, loaded with passengers bound for the springs, soon drove up and stopped at the same house, which was the regular place of dining for the passengers. After dinner I rode on to the springs, keeping along the most of the way in company with the stage. My Jenny attracted very marked attention from the driver and passengers. The driver especially was profuse in his expressions of admiration. As I rode up to the hotel, the listless, lounging visitors, who were so deep in the Brush that they had very little to attract or interest them, regarded her gait and movements with general attention and delight. When I dismounted, a black boy was soon in my saddle, and my Jenny moved off to the stable with her usual fleetness and grace. I entered the hotel and registered my name, without any prefix or suffix to indicate my employment or profession. The weather was very hot, the roads very dusty, and after the fashion of the country I was at once furnished with water to wash. As I stood wiping myself, the stage-driver rushed into the room and up to me in great excitement and said :

"Mr. Pierson, will you allow your horse to run? The money is up and we'll have a race if you'll only allow her to run"—at the same time holding up and shaking in my face a mass of bills that were drawn through his fingers, after the fashion of gamblers in those parts. I was startled to hear my name pronounced in a strange place, and by a stranger, but in a moment bethought me that he had learned it by looking on the hotel-register. I was more startled by the strangeness of the proposition. As the servant stood with my saddle-bags on his arm, waiting to show me to my room, I answered perhaps a little too abruptly, "No, sir," and followed him to my room, to prepare for supper. When the supper-bell rang, and I stepped out of my room upon the piazza, a portly man of gentlemanly bear-

ing, who had evidently taken his position there to wait
for me, approached me pleasantly and said:

"I hope, sir, you will reconsider your decision and
allow your mare to run. As soon as you rode up I
offered to bet two hundred and fifty dollars that she
would outrun anything here, and the money is up.
Allow me to say that I am an old Virginian, and a judge
of horses, and if you will let her run I am sure to win."

By this time I had entirely recovered my self-posses-
sion, and, bowing politely, I looked directly into his eyes
and said:

"Do you think, sir, it will do for a Presbyterian
clergyman to commence horse-racing *so soon* after reaching the Springs?"

He was as much startled as I had been—in fact, so
startled that he could not say a word, and I left him
without any reply, and went in to supper. When I returned from the dining-room I found him at the door,
and he approached me in the most subdued and respectful manner and said:

"Allow me to speak to you again, sir. I wish to
apologize, sir; I beg your pardon, sir; I assure you, sir,
that nothing would induce me knowingly to insult a
clergyman."

I responded, very pleasantly:

"I am certain, sir, that no insult was intended, and
therefore there is no pardon to be granted."

He thanked me very warmly for my kind construction of his motives, and left me with a lighter step and brighter face. His companions were all greatly pleased with my treatment of the matter; and, as I have elsewhere said, there was a general turnout of all the gamblers—of whom he was one of the most prominent—to hear me preach in the ballroom the next Sabbath. But I need not say, to any one at all familiar with life in the Southwest, that he had to "stand treat" all around among his companions, for being thus, in the vernacular of the country, "picked up" by the preacher.

In passing through another part of this county the following winter, I rode up to a blacksmith-shop to get a shoe tightened. As soon as the blacksmith came out he said:

"Wasn't you at the Springs last summer with this mare?"

I replied in the affirmative, and, on looking at him, recognized the man that kept a little shop there, and had shod her in the summer.

"Well," said he, leaning upon her neck, patting her affectionately, and looking into vacancy with a pleased expression, as if living over some pleasant scene in the past, "they got her out, preacher, and run her, any way." And then, as if to make the matter all right with me, he looked up into my face and said, with the most satisfied smile and emphatic nod: "And, preacher, she beat, she did. He won his money!"

During my vacation-trips to the East, for several summers, I left my horse with some kind, warm friends upon a plantation, for the ladies and children to ride as they might wish. At first it was difficult for me to make satisfactory arrangements to leave her for several weeks. I could not trust her at a livery-stable. There I felt sure she would get a great many stolen rides. I found also that the temptation was too great for the virtue of some professed friends with whom I left her, for on my return I found she had been overridden, and looked worn rather than rested from the vacation I had intended for her as well as myself. But in my travels I found a lady from my native State, New York, who had gone South as a teacher, and married a planter. There was a slight disparity in their ages. I would not take oath as to the exact difference, but I heard a good many times that, when married, she was nineteen and he forty-nine. If that was so, the marriage furnished confirmation of the popular talk and notions concerning "an old man's darling." He was certainly as kind and indulgent as a husband could well be. She was a Presbyterian and he a Baptist. He was kind and genial, and full of vivacity and life, and loved to entertain me as his "wife's preacher," and for her sake, as well as to gratify his own warm social instincts. Here, at each return for years, I ever found the warmest welcome and the kindest home. To her my visits were like those of an old friend, for, when far away from the companions and scenes of early life, the ties that unite

3

those from the same State become strong and endearing. But far stronger than this is the bond that unites members of different churches to their own clergymen, and especially when they but rarely enjoy their ministrations. Gifted, intelligent, and full of energy, and also sympathizing deeply with the object of my Christian toils and labors, she spared no pains to make her house what it ever was to me, a delightful resting-place and home. A large, fine chamber always awaited me, to which they gave my name, and here I spent many delightful hours. I brought to them many tales of my adventures in the Brush, for which my host had the keenest appreciation, and I heard from him many accounts of preachers and preaching he had known and heard that are hard to be surpassed, which I intend to give my readers in another chapter. It was with these friends that for years I left my horse during all my vacation-journeys. Here she became a family pet. Here I was sure she would never be overridden, and always receive the kindest care. Here she came to be regarded with an attachment, if possible, greater than my own; for, when I returned for her, the children would have a hearty cry as I rode her away. When at length I closed my labors in the Southwest and left the region, my kind Baptist friend was more than glad to procure her for his Presbyterian wife, and I left her where I was sure she would have the kindest treatment while serviceable, and enjoy a comfortable and honored old age.

CHAPTER IV.

THE hospitality extended to ministers of the gospel by the people who lived in the Brush was generous and large-hearted to a degree that I have never known among any other class of people. They obeyed the Scripture injunction, "Use hospitality without grudging." They were "not forgetful to entertain strangers." I found their tables, their beds, their stables, and indeed all the comforts of their rude homes, always open for the rest and refreshment of myself and my indispensable horse. We were as welcome to all these as to the water that bubbled from their springs and "ran among the hills."

At the commencement of my itinerant life, on leaving the families where I had spent a night or taken a meal, I used to propose to pay them, and ask for my bill; but I found this gave offense. Many seemed to regard it as a reflection on their generosity for me to intimate or suppose that they would take pay for entertaining a preacher. I therefore adopted a formula that saved me from all danger of wounding their feelings, and relieved my character from all suspicion of a disposition to avoid the payment of my bills. It was as follows: When about to leave a family, I said to them, "I am indebted to you for a night's entertainment," to which the general response was: "Not at all, sir. Come and stay with us again, whenever you pass this way."

It was a very rare occurrence that I was permitted to cancel my indebtedness by paying for what I had received.

In thanking them for their hospitality, as of course I always did on leaving them, they made me feel that I had conferred a favor rather than incurred an obli-gation by staying with them.

For years it was my custom to apply for entertainment at any house wherever night overtook me, and I invariably received a cordial welcome. This application for entertainment was always made according to the custom of the people, and in their own vernacular, which I will illustrate by an example.

In my horseback-journeyings I had reached the tall, dense, heavy forests of the bottom-lands of the Mississippi River, about a dozen miles from the Father of Waters. As the sun was about setting, I came upon a large "dead'ning," where the underbrush had been cut out and burned off, the large trees had been girdled and had died, and a crop of corn had been raised among the dead forest-trees, before the new-comer in this wilderness had been able to completely clear a field around his newly-erected log-cabin. Turning off from the corduroy-road upon which I had been traveling, I took a footpath, and, following that, was soon as near the cabin as a high rail-fence would allow me to approach on horseback. A short distance from this log-cabin was a still smaller one occupied by a colored aunty and her family, and used for a kitchen; and not far off still another log-building, used for a barn and stable.

The most of my readers in the older sections of the country will suppose that I had now only to dismount, hitch my horse, climb the fence, rap at the door, and so gain admittance to my resting-place for the night. Far otherwise. Only the most untraveled and inexperienced in the Brush would undertake so rash an experiment.

Sitting upon my horse, I called out in a loud voice, "Hello there!" That call was for the same purpose that the city pastor mounts the stone steps and rings the bell at the door of his parishioner. It was rather more effective.

A large pack of hounds and various other kinds of dogs responded with a barking chorus, a group of black pickaninnies rushed from the adjacent kitchen, followed to the door by their sable mother, with arms a-kimbo and hands fresh from mixing the pone or corn-dodger for the family supper; all, with distended eyes and mouth, and shining ivory, staring at the stranger with excited and pleased curiosity. At almost the same instant, the mistress of the incipient plantation approached the door of her cabin, stockingless and shoeless, with a dress of woolsey woven in her own loom by her own hands, and cut and made by her own skill, with face not less pleased and excited than the others, and her cordial greeting of · "How d'y, stranger—how d'y, sir? 'Light, sir! [alight]—'light, sir!"

Remaining upon my horse, I replied: "I am a stranger in these parts, madam. I have ridden about fifty miles since morning and am very tired. Can I get to stay with you to-night, madam?"

"Oh, yes," she replied, promptly, "if you can put up with our rough fare. We never turn anybody away."

I told her I should be very glad to stay with her, and dismounted. The dogs, who would otherwise have resisted my approach to the door by a combined attack, obeyed their instructions not to harm me, and granted me a safe entrance as a recognized friend.

Such was the universal training of the dogs, and such the uniform method of approaching and gaining admittance to the houses of the people in the Brush. My hostess informed me that her husband was at work in the "dead'ning," but that he would soon be at home and take care of my horse.

I told her that I could do that myself, and she

sent her little son along with me to the stable, where I bestowed that kind and, I may say, affectionate care that one who journeys for years on horseback learns to bestow upon his faithful horse. I then entered the cabin, and received that warm welcome that awaits the traveler in our Western wilds.

Shall I describe my home for the night? It was a new log-house, less than twenty feet square, and advanced to a state of completeness beyond many in which I had lodged, inasmuch as the large openings between the logs had been filled with "chink and daubing." The chimney, built upon the outside of the house, was made of split sticks, laid up in the proper form, and thoroughly "daubed" with mud, so as to prevent them from taking fire. A large opening cut through the logs communicated with this chimney, and formed the ample fireplace. The roof was made of "shakes"—pieces of timber rived out very much in the form of staves, but not shaved at all. These were laid upon the roof like shingles, except that they were not nailed on, but "weighted on " — kept in their places by small timbers laid across each row of "shakes" over the entire roof. These timbers were kept in their places by shorter ones placed between them, transversely, up and down the roof. In this manner the pioneer constructs a roof for his cabin, by his own labor, without the expenditure of a dime for nails. With wooden hinges and a wooden latch for his door, he needs to purchase little but glass for his windows, to provide a comfortable home for his family. His latch-string, made of hemp or flax that he has raised, or from the skin of the deer which he has pursued and slain in the chase, which, as the old song has it—

"Hangs outside the door,"

symbolizes the cordial welcome and abounding hospitality to be found within.

At the end of the room opposite the fireplace there was a bed in each corner, under one of which there was a "trundle-bed" for the children. There was no chamber-floor or chamber above to obstruct the view of the roof. There was no division into apartments, not even by hanging up blankets, a device I have seen resorted to in less primitive regions. From floor to roof, from wall to wall, all was a single "family" room, which was evidently to be occupied by the family and myself in common. A rough board table, some plain chairs, and a very few other articles completed the inventory of household furniture of the pioneer's home to which I had been welcomed.

Such a home was the birthplace of Lincoln, and many other of the greatest, wisest, and best men that have ever blessed our country. Such homes have been crowned with abundance, and have been the scenes of as much real comfort and joy as any others in our land.

I have found that curiosity is a trait that is not monopolized by any one section of country or class of people. It belongs to all localities, and to all grades and kinds of people. I therefore, in accordance with what a pretty wide experience had taught me was the best course to pursue, proceeded at once to gratify the curiosity of my hostess as to who her guest was, and what business had brought him to this wild region. I told her my name, and that I was a Presbyterian preacher, and an agent of the American Bible Society. This not only satisfied her curiosity, but was very gratifying information to her, and I received a renewed and cordial welcome to her home as a minister of the gospel.

In the course of the ordinary conversation and questions that attend such a meeting of strangers in the Brush, I learned that she and her husband had emigrated from a county some hundreds of miles east, which I had several times visited in the prosecution of my mission, and I was able to give her a great deal of information in regard to her old neighbors and friends. We were in the midst of an earnest conversation in regard to these people, when her husband came in from his labors. On being introduced to me, and informed in regard to my mission, he repeated the welcome his wife had already given me to the hospitality of their cabin.

Our supper was such as is almost universally spread

in the wilds of the Southwest. It consisted of an abundance of hot corn-bread, fried bacon, potatoes, and coffee. A hard day's labor and a long day's ride prepared us to do it equal justice.

The evening wore rapidly away in conversation. Such pioneers are not dull, stupid men. Their peculiar life gives activity to mind as well as body. My host was anxious and glad to hear from the great outside active world, with which I had more recently mingled, and had questions to ask and views to give as to what was going on in the political and religious world.

At length our wearied bodies made a plea for rest that could not be refused, and I was invited to conduct their family worship. This invitation was extended in the language and manner peculiar to the Southern and Southwestern sections of the country. This is universally as follows:

The Bible and hymn-book are brought forward by the host, and laid upon the table or stand, when he turns to the preacher and says, "Will you take the books, sir?"

That is the invitation to lead the devotions of the family in singing and prayer. It has been my happy lot to receive and respond to that invitation—as I did that night—in many hundreds of families and in some of the wildest portions of our land.

The method of extending an invitation to "ask a

blessing" before a meal is quite as peculiar. Being seated at the table, the host, turning to the preacher, says, "Will you make a beginning, sir?"—all at table reverently bowing their heads as he extends the invitation, and while the blessing is being asked.

So, too, I have "made a beginning" at many a hospitable board in many different States. I did not that night make the mistake that is reported of an inexperienced home-missionary explorer, in similar circumstances, who, laboring under the impression that "to retire" and "to go to bed" were synonymous terms, said, "Madam, I will retire, if you please."

"Retire!" she rejoined; "we never retires, stranger. We just goes to bed."

Sitting with the family before the large fireplace, I said, "Madam, I have ridden a long distance to-day, and am very tired."

"You can go to bed at any time you wish, sir," said she. "Just take the left-hand bed."

I withdrew behind their backs to "lay my garments by," took the left-hand bed, turned my face to the left-hand wall, and slept soundly for the night.

When I awoke in the morning, husband and wife had arisen and left the room, he to feed his team, and she to attend to her household duties in the kitchen. After an early breakfast, and again leading their family devotions, I bade them good-by, with many thanks for their kindness, and with repeated invitations on

their part to be sure to spend the night with them
should I ever come that way again. But I have never
seen them since.

I have very often recalled a hospitable reception in
the Brush, of a very different character, the recollection of which has always been exceedingly pleasant to
me. Wishing to visit a rough, wild, remote region, at
a season of the year when the roads were almost im-
passable on account of the spring rains and the mud,
I concluded to go the greater part of the distance by
steamboats, down one river and up another, and then
ride about fifty miles in a stage or mail-wagon. The
roads would scarcely be called roads at all in most
parts of the country, and I shall not be able to give
to many of my readers any true idea of the exceeding
roughness of that ride. A considerable part of the way
was through the bottom-lands of one of the smaller
Southwestern rivers that swell the volume of the Mississippi. A recent freshet had left the high-water mark
upon the trees several feet higher than the backs of
our horses; and as we jolted over the small stumps
and great roots of the trees, from which the earth had
been washed away by the freshet, I was wearied, exceedingly wearied, by the rough road and comfortless
vehicle in which I traveled.

At length we came upon a very pleasant plantation, with a comfortable house and surroundings, where
the driver, a boy about fifteen years old, told me he

would feed his team, and we would get our dinner. It was not an hotel. Mail-contractors in this region often make such arrangements to procure feed for their horses and meals for the few passengers that they carry, at private houses. As I entered the house I was greeted with one of those calm, mild, sweet faces that one never forgets. I should think that my hostess was between thirty-five and forty years old. I was too weary to engage in much conversation, and she was quiet, and said very little to me. As I observed her movements about the room in preparing the dinner, I thought I had never seen a face that presented a more perfect picture of contentment and peace. I felt perfectly sure that she was a Christian—that her face bespoke "the peace of God that passeth all understanding." When she invited the driver and myself to take seats at the table, I said, "Shall I ask a blessing, madam?"

With a smile she bowed assent, and, as I concluded and looked up, her face was all radiant with joy, and she said excitedly, "You are a preacher, sir!"

I replied, "Yes, madam."

"Well," she responded, "I am glad to see you. I love to see preachers. I love to cook for them, and take care of them. I love to have them in my house."

I told her who I was, explained the character of my mission, and expressed, I trust with becoming warmth, my gratification at the cordiality of her welcome.

"Oh," said she, "if I was a man, I know what I would do. I would do nothing but preach. I'd go, and go, and go; and preach, and preach, and preach. I wouldn't have anything to pester me. I wouldn't marry nary woman in the world. I'd go, and go, and go—and preach, and preach, and preach, until I could preach no longer; and then I'd lie down—close my eyes—and—go on."

Was there ever a more graphic and truthful description of an earnest, apostolic life? Was there ever a more simple, beautiful description of a peaceful Christian death? They recall the statement of Paul, "This *one thing* I do"; and the story of Stephen, "And when he had said this, he fell asleep."

The people who have spent their lives deep in the Brush, as this good woman had, have no other idea of a preacher of the gospel but one whose duty and mission it is to "go" and "preach." They have been accustomed to hearing but one message, or at most a few messages, from their lips, and then hear their farewell words, listen to their farewell songs, shake hands with them, and see them take their departure to "go" and "preach" to others who, like them, dwell in lone and solitary wilds. Meetings and partings like these have originated and given their peculiar power to such refrains as—

"Say, brothers, will you meet us—
Say, brothers, will you meet us—

Say, brothers, will you meet us
On Canaan's happy shore?

"By the grace of God we'll meet you—
By the grace of God we'll meet you—
By the grace of God we'll meet you
On Canaan's happy shore."

This woman knew little of the great world—had little that it calls culture; her language was that of the people among whom she lived, and was such as she had always been accustomed to hear; but her thoughts were deep and pure, her "peace flowed like a river," and her communion with God lifted her to companionship with the noblest and best of earth. Though I spent but little more than an hour in her presence, and many years have passed since that transient meeting, her picture still hangs in the chamber of my memory, calm, pure, and saintly, and breathing upon my spirit a perpetual benediction.

CHAPTER V.

RELIGIOUS meetings, popularly denominated " basket-meetings," were known and recognized as established institutions in the Brush. They were among the assemblages that had resulted from the sparseness of the population in those regions. Where the country was hilly and mountainous, and the settlers were scattered along the streams in the narrow valleys; or the land was so rough and poor that only occasional patches would reward tillage; or for various other causes, the families were but few, and far distant from each other, it was a very difficult matter for the people to leave their homes day after day to attend a continuous meeting. Hence, among other religious gatherings, they had long been accustomed to hold what were called basket-meetings.

These meetings involved less labor and trouble than camp-meetings, and could often be held where such a meeting would be impossible. They were usually not as large, and did not continue as many days.

They were called "basket-meetings" from the fact
that those from a distance brought their provisions,
already cooked, in large baskets, and in quantities
sufficient to last them during the continuance of the
meeting. They put up no tents or cabins on the
ground. They did not cook or sleep there. They
most frequently commenced on Saturday, and continued through the Sabbath. They generally had a prayer-
meeting and preaching on Saturday forenoon, and then
adjourned for an hour or two. During this intermission the greater part of the people dispersed in groups
among the trees, and took their dinner after the manner of a picnic. Those living in the immediate vicinity returned to their homes for dinner, taking with
them as many of those in attendance as they could
possibly secure. Every stranger was sure of repeated
invitations to dine, both with these families and neighborhood groups among the trees, and at the adjacent
cabins. After dinner they reassembled and had a repetition of the services of the morning.

Unlike a camp-meeting, they had no services at
night. When the afternoon meetings were concluded,
the people dispersed and spent the night at the cabins
within two or three miles around. All the people in
these cabins usually kept open house upon such an
occasion. They were present, and, after the benediction
was pronounced, they mounted the stumps and logs
and extended a general invitation to any present to

spend the night with them. Not satisfied with giving
this general invitation, they jumped down and went
among the rapidly dispersing crowd and followed it
with private personal solicitations to accept their prof-
fered hospitality.

On the Sabbath, they reassembled with augmented
numbers, and the services of Saturday were reënacted,
with such additions and variations as the circumstances
might demand.

The first basket-meeting that I ever attended was
so new and strange to me in all its incidents, that,
though many years have intervened, my recollections
of it are as vivid as though it had occurred but yesterday. It was in a very rough, wild region. The
country had been settled a long time, so that those in
attendance were genuine backwoods people "to the
manner born." The place of meeting was in a tall,
dense, unbroken forest. The underbrush had been cut
and cleared away, a few trees had been so felled that
rude planks, made by splitting logs, could be placed
across them for seats for the ladies, while the men
mostly sat upon the trunks of other fallen trees. The
pulpit or "stand" for the preacher was original and
truly Gothic in its construction. It was made by cut-
ting horizontal notches immediately opposite to each
other, in the sides of two large oak-trees, standing
about four feet apart, and inserting into these notches
a board about a foot wide, that had been placed across

a wagon and used for a seat by some of those present in coming to the meeting. The preacher placed his Bible and hymn-book upon this board, hung the indispensable saddle-bags in which he had brought them across one end of it, and so was ready for the services. I thought I had never seen in any cathedral a pulpit more simple and grand. Those towering, grand old oaks, with their massive, outstretching branches, spoke eloquently of the power and grandeur of the God who made them. And yet, small and puny as the preacher appeared in the contrast, it was a fitting place for him to stand and proclaim his message to the people who worshiped beneath them. Comparatively unlearned and ignorant as he was, he could tell them from that open Bible what they would never learn in the contemplation of grand old forests, or stars, or suns, or all the sublimest works of nature. All these are mute and dumb in regard to the story of the cross. However they may enkindle our rapture, or excite our reverence, they will never tell us how sin may be forgiven —how the soul may be saved.

The indispensable matter in the selection of grounds for a basket-meeting or a camp-meeting in the Southwest was a good spring of clear, running water. This must be so large as to furnish an abundance of water, not only for all the people who would be present, but for all the horses necessary to transport themselves and their provisions to the place of meeting. In hot weather the demands for water were large, and there was need for a "clear spring" like that so beautifully described by the poet Bryant:

> ". . . yon clear spring, that, midst its herbs,
> Wells softly forth, and wandering, steeps the roots
> Of half the mighty forest."

The sermon on this occasion was plain, sensible, and earnest. The preacher was superior to the people, and yet in all respects one of them. He had been born in the Brush, raised in the Brush, and had spent many years in preaching to the people in the Brush. He dressed as they dressed, talked as they talked, and, unconsciously to himself, used all their provincialisms in his sermons. In his thoughts, feelings, and manner of life he was in full sympathy with them. He had toiled among them long, earnestly, and successfully. He had preached to a great many congregations, scattered over a wide extent of Brush country. He had been associated with his brethren of different denominations in holding a great many union basket-meetings similar to the one now in progress. He was widely known, beloved, and honored. Perhaps the most widely known, honored, and successful pastorate in the country has been that of the late Rev. Dr. Gardner Spring, in New York. But I do not think that Dr. Spring, with all his talents, culture, and learning, could possibly have been as useful, as successful, as honored among these people, as was this preacher. He could not have eaten their coarse food, slept in their wretched beds, mingled with them in their daily life, or been in such complete sympathy with them in their poverty, struggles, temptations, and modes of thought, as to have so won their love and reverence, and led them in such numbers to the cross of Christ. "There are diversity of gifts, but the same spirit," etc. I honor these noble and heroic workers in the Master's vineyard, who thus toil on in the Brush, through scores of years, all unknown to fame. Many of them know nothing of Latin, Greek, and Hebrew, but they know how to win souls to Christ, and the highest authority has said, "He that winneth souls is wise."

That congregation, when assembled, seated, and engaged in their devotions, presented a scene not to be forgotten. The preacher, small in stature, stood upon a rude platform at the feet of the massive columns of his pulpit. The people were seated among the standing trees, upon seats arranged without any of the usual regularity and order, but lying at all points of the compass just as they had been able to fall, the smaller trees among the larger ones. The voice of prayer and song ascended amid those massive, towering columns, crowned with arches formed by their outstretching branches, and covered with dense foliage. It was the worship of God in his own temple. It carried the thoughts back to many scenes not unlike it, in the lives and labors of Christ and his apostles, when they preached and taught upon the Mount of Olives, by the shores of Gennesaret, and over the hills and valleys of Palestine. It gave new force and beauty to the familiar words of Bryant's grand and noble " Forest Hymn : "

> " The groves were God's first temples, ere man learned
> To hew the shaft and lay the architrave,
> And spread the roof above them—ere he framed
> The lofty vault, to gather and roll back
> The sound of anthems ; in the darkling wood,
> Amid the cool and silence, he knelt down,
> And offered to the Mightiest solemn thanks
> And supplication. . . .
> . . . . Be it ours to meditate,
> In these calm shades, thy milder majesty,
> And to the beautiful order of thy works
> Learn to conform the order of our lives."

At the conclusion of the morning sermon the greater part of the congregation dispersed among the trees to take their dinner in the manner I have already described. I was invited to go with the preacher to a cabin about a mile distant, where we were to have our home during the meeting. We mounted our horses and accompanied our host through the woods to his residence. As I looked back; I saw that we were followed by some forty or more other guests. On reaching his home I found three buildings—a log-house, log-kitchen, and log-stable. Our horses were put in the stable and bountifully fed with corn in the ear and fodder. "Fodder" in these regions has a limited signification, and is applied only to the leaves which are stripped from the corn-stalks, tied in small bundles, and generally stacked for preservation. The stalks are not cut, as in the North and East, but the leaves are stripped from them while standing. This is the usual feed for horses in the place of hay.

The house was similar to all log-houses, but, as our company was so numerous, I had the curiosity to ask our host how large it was, and he told me that he cut the logs just twenty feet long. Its single room was, therefore, less than twenty feet square. We, however, received a warm and cordial welcome, and host, hostess, and guests seemed exceedingly happy. With a part of the company, I was soon invited into the adjoining house to dinner. This was much smaller—not more than ten or fifteen feet square. A loom in one corner filled a large part of the room. This was a very important part of their household treasures, as the greater portion of the clothing of the entire family was woven upon it. A long, narrow table, of home construction, occupied the space between the foot of the loom and the wall. There was a large fireplace in front, before which the coffee was smoking. A chair at each end and a bench on each side of the table furnished seats for ten guests. Our bill of fare was cold barbecued shoat, sweet potatoes roasted in the ashes, bread, honey,

and coffee. Our honey was from a "bee tree," and
our bread was of the Graham variety, from the neces-
sities of the case. The wheat had been ground at a
"horse mill" in the neighborhood, where they had
no arrangements for separating the bran from the
flour. Such a dinner was not to be despised by
hungry men. By the way, I have found that over a
very wide extent of our country the *men*, on such
occasions, always eat first and alone, the women meanwhile standing around the table and waiting upon
them. After we had finished our dinner, the table
was rapidly reset by the aid of the "sisters" present,
and ten more guests took their seats and dined. The
same course was repeated until the table was set five
times, and fifty persons had dined bountifully in that
little log-cabin.

Having all dined, we returned to the preaching
"stand," and the congregation reassembled. I preached
to them at 4 P. M., and all the services were conducted
to the close in a manner not essentially different from
preaching services elsewhere.

The audience was dismissed for the night, and dispersed among the nearest cabins. My clerical friend
and myself were joined by a young licentiate, and returned to spend the night at the house at which we
had dined. The company was not as large as that at
dinner, but to one inexperienced in such life, as I
then was, it was beyond my comprehension how they

could be entertained for the night. My experience and observation at dinner had shown me how we could get through with our supper. A succession of tables I understood, but how could that be applied to sleeping arrangements? A succession of beds was a kind of "succession" I had never heard or read of in ecclesiastical or any other history. But my perplexities were evidently not felt by any one else in the company, and I dismissed them.

All seemed as happy as they could well be. Conversation was animated. All tongues were loosed. There were stories of former basket and other meetings, of wonderful revivals, and of remarkable conversions. There were reminiscences of eccentric and favorite preachers who had labored among them long years before. There was the greatest variety of *real* Western and Southwestern religious melodies and songs. These were interspersed with the conversation during the evening, and were the source of great and unfailing interest and joy. So the hours rolled on, and all were happy. It was the occasion to which they had looked forward, and for which they had planned for months—the great occasion of all the year, and it brought no disappointment. For myself, I must say that if I ever drew upon my stores of anecdote, and whatever powers of entertaining I may possess, it was upon this occasion. I was quite in sympathy with the general joy and good feeling. During

4

the evening one and another had called for the singing of different religious songs that were their favorites. On such occasions there was a general appeal
to a young lady, who was quite the best singer in the
company, to know if she knew the song called for;
and if she did it was sung. At length a hymn was
called for, and in response to the usual appeal she
said she did not know it. I opened a book, found the
hymn and tune, handed it to her, and said, "Here is
the hymn with the tune. Perhaps you can sing it."

She declined to take the book, saying, with the
utmost frankness, "Oh! sir, I can't read."

I now learned to my amazement that all the
hymns and tunes she had sung that evening she had
learned by rote—learned by hearing them sung by
others. She was a young lady, some eighteen or
twenty years old, of more than common beauty of
face and form, and yet she had no hesitation at all
in revealing the fact that she could not read. I afterward received a similar shock on remarking to a
young lady that I met at a county-seat, whose home
I had previously visited, "I understand that a number
of the young ladies in your neighborhood can not
read."

"Oh!" said she, "there are only two young ladies
there that can read."

I afterward visited many neighborhoods where it
was as proper to ask a young lady if she could read

as it was to ask for a drink of water, the time of day, or any other question.

At length the evening passed, and the hour for rest and sleep came. One of our number "took the books" and led our evening devotions. A chapter was read, our final hymn was sung, and we all bowed in prayer around that family altar. As we arose from our knees, the brethren present all walked out of doors. The sisters remained within. Some "Martha" among them had enumerated our company. There were three beds in the cabin. These were divided, and a sufficient number of beds made up on the bedsteads and over the cabin-floor to furnish a sleeping-place for all our company. This accomplished, some signal—I know not what—was given, and the brethren' returned to the house. I followed them. The sisters were all in bed, upon the bedsteads, with their heads covered up by the blankets. We got into our beds as though these blankets had been thick walls. Our numbers in this room included three young ladies, a man and his wife and child, and six other men.

When we awoke in the morning some of the brethren engaged in conversation for a time, until Mr. W——, the preacher, remarked, "I suppose it is time to think about getting up."

At this signal the sisters covered their heads again with their blankets, and we arose, dressed, and departed. My companion for the night was the young

licentiate; and as we walked toward the stable to look
after our horses—the first thing usually done in the
morning by persons journeying on horseback—I remarked to him, "Last night has been something new
in my experience. I never slept in that way before."

He looked at me with an expression of the profoundest astonishment, and exclaimed, "You haven't!"

I said no more. I saw that I was the verdant one.
I was the only one in all the company to whom the
experiences of the night suggested a thought of anything unusual or strange. So trite and true it is that
"one half of the world does not know how the other
half lives."

The Sabbath was the "great day of the feast." It
brought together some three or four hundred people—
a very large congregation in such a sparsely settled
country. I made an address to them in the morning,
explaining the extended operations of the American
Bible Society in our own and other lands. I told
them that the Society was then attempting to place
a copy of the Word of God in every family in our
country; that Mr. K——, a venerable and honored
class-leader, had been appointed to canvass their
county; and that either by sale or gift he would supply every family in the county with the Bible that
would receive it. All of these facts were new to the
most of them, and were listened to with the greatest
interest. Large numbers of them had no Bibles in

their families; they were more than sixty miles from a book-store, which many of them never visited, and they were glad to have the Bible brought to their own doors, and furnished to them at so small a price. By making these statements I gave the Bible-distributor an introduction to the people scattered over a wide extent of country, which prepared them to welcome him to their families and greatly facilitated his labors.

My brief address was followed by a sermon entirely different from those of the preacher I have already described, and deserves notice as a type of thousands that are preached to the people in the Brush. Scarcely a sentence in the sermon was uttered in the usual method of speech. It was drawled out in a sing-song tone from the beginning to the end. The preacher ran his voice up, and sustained it at so high a pitch that he could make but little variation of voice upward. The air in his lungs would become exhausted, and at the conclusion of every sentence he would "catch" his breath with an "ah." As he proceeded with his sermon, and his vocal organs became wearied with this most unnatural exertion, the "ah" was repeated more and more frequently, until, with the most painful contortions of face and form, he would with difficulty articulate, in his sing-song tone:

"Oh, my beloved brethren—ah, and sisters—ah, you have all got to die—ah, and be buried—ah, and go to the judgment—ah, and stand before the great white throne—ah, and receive your rewards—ah, for the deeds —ah, done in the body—ah."

From the beginning to the end of his sermon, which occupied just an hour and ten minutes by my watch, I could not see the slightest evidence that he had any idea what he was going to say from one sentence to another. While "catching his breath," and saying "ah," he seemed to determine what he would say next. There was no more train of thought or connection of ideas than in the harangue of a maniac. And yet many hundreds of such sermons are preached in the Brush, and I am sorry to add that thousands of the people had rather hear these sermons than any others. This "holy tone" has charms for them not possessed by any possible eloquence. As the preacher "warms up" and becomes more animated in the progress of his discourse, the more impressible sisters begin to move their heads and bodies, and soon all the devout brethren and sisters sway their bodies back and forth in perfect unison, keeping time, in some mysterious manner, to his singsong tone.

It seemed sad to me that such a congregation, gathered from such long distances, should have the morning hour occupied with such a sermon. But it was a union meeting, the preacher was the representative of his denomination, and they would have gone away worse than disappointed—grievously outraged—if they could not have heard this sermon with the "holy tone."

But our basket-meeting was to be signalized by an incident always interesting in all countries, in all grades of society, among the most rustic as well as among the most refined. After the benediction, a part of the congregation who were in the secret remained upon their seats, casting knowing and pleasant glances at each other. My friend W——, who, like a good many other preachers, and some preachers' wives, had faithfully kept a secret that a good many were "just dying to know," took his position in front of the "stand." A trembling, blushing, but happy pair advanced from the crowd, and took their position before him. The groom produced from his pocket the indispensable license. The dispersing crowd, having by some electric influence been apprised of what was going on, came rushing back, and mounted the surrounding stumps and logs, forming a standing background to the sitting circle. All looked on and listened in silence, while the preacher in a strong, clear voice proceeded to solemnize the marriage and pronounce them husband and wife. The scene was strange and strikingly impressive. It seemed a wedding in Nature's own cathedral. The day was perfect. Some rays from the sun penetrated the dense foliage above and fell upon the scene, mingling golden hues with the shadows, as the poet, the recently deceased A. B. Street, has so beautifully described:

" Here showers the sun in golden dots,
    Here rests the shade in ebon spots,
    So blended that the very air
    Seems network as I enter here."

After the usual congratulations and kisses the groom withdrew, and reappeared in a few moments mounted upon a large gray horse. The bride, having gained the top of a stump, mounted his horse behind him, and the two rode away, as happy and satisfied as they could well be.

The larger congregation of the Sabbath made larger demands upon their hospitality; but these demands were fully met. The dinner, both under the trees and at the cabins, was but a reënactment of the scenes of the day before on an enlarged scale.

In the afternoon Mr. W—— preached a sensible and earnest sermon, like that of the day before. In my pocket-diary, written at the time, I have characterized it as a "thundering sermon." His voice was strong, and capable of reaching the largest congregations that he addressed in the open air. This sermon concluded the services of the basket-meeting. As the benediction was pronounced, three gentlemen on horseback arrived upon the ground. They were a presiding elder, a circuit-rider, and a class-leader, on their way to conference. They had preached some fifteen miles away in the morning, and continued their journey to reach this meeting. I knew them all, and had preached with and for them at their homes. As they were strangers to most, if not all, the people, I introduced them to the clergymen and others present. They were some twenty miles from any hotel or public-house, and of course must spend the night with some of these people. My host, to whom I had introduced them, said:

"I should be very glad to have you all stay with me, but I can't take care of your horses. I have a plenty of houseroom, but my stable is full."

From what I have already said of the numbers who dined and lodged with him, it will be seen that he had very enlarged ideas of the capacity of his house. An enthusiastic neighbor, who was about as rough a looking specimen of a backwoodsman as I ever saw, stepped forward and said:

"I have room enough for your horses and you too. I should be glad to have you all go with me."

The presiding elder went with him, but the preacher and the class-leader were claimed by others.

Before leaving the grounds, it was arranged between us that we should all meet at a designated place in the morning, and I would travel with them to the conference, to which I was thus far on my way. Though not an Arminian, but a Calvinist, though not a Methodist, but a Presbyterian, I knew that a cordial welcome awaited me as a representative of the American Bible Society. I knew that, in addition to this official welcome, I should

receive the warm greetings of brethren beloved, with
whom I had traveled many hundreds of miles over their
"circuits," and mingled in all the novel, interesting, and
eventful scenes in their wild itinerant life.   When I met
the elder the next morning, I asked him the nature of
the very ample accommodations that were offered him.
He said he slept upon the floor, but he did not undertake to count the number who shared it with him.

So ended the various incidents of our basket-meeting ; but the recollection of it has been among the pleasant memories of my life in the Brush.

SOME EXPLANATORY WORDS.

Perhaps some statement in explanation of this
" rough " but abounding hospitality of the people in the
Brush is demanded in justice to those persons and
places whose hospitality would seem to suffer in the
contrast.   I might enumerate many circumstances connected with life in a wild, unsettled country that will
occur to most readers as the cause of this abounding
hospitality ; but it seems to me that the *chief* reason
is the fact that meat, bread, and all their provisions,
excepting groceries, cost them so very little.   They estimate what they can use scarcely more than the water
taken from their springs.   Beef, pork, and bread cost
them almost nothing.   Their cattle run at large, and
their free range includes thousands of acres of unoccu-

pied lands. They grow and increase in this manner
with but little attention or care. The hogs find their
food in the woods the greater part of the year, and in
the fall they fatten upon the nuts or "mast." The oak,
hickory, beech, and other trees that abound in these
extensive forests afford vast quantities of these nuts,
which these people claim for their own hogs, whoever
may own the land. I knew a man that owned several
thousand acres of these lands, who sold the nuts on the
ground to a "speculator," who drove his hogs upon the
tract of land to eat them. But the residents were in-
censed at this trespass upon their immemorial privileges,
and secretly shot and killed so many of these hogs that
their owner was glad to escape with any part of his
drove, and leave them possessors of the "mast." The
method by which these people retain and recognize their
ownership in the hogs that run at large and mingle together in the woods was quite new to me. The owner
looks carefully after the young pigs, calls them, and
feeds them, for some days or weeks, until they know his
voice, and will come at his call. Whatever kind of a
hoot, scream, or yell it is, they learn to associate it with
their food, and run at the sound. Sometimes the owner
merely blows a horn. If a hundred hogs belonging
to half a dozen men are feeding together in the woods,
and their owners sound their calls from different hills,
the hogs will separate and rush in the direction of the
sound to which they have been accustomed. In this

manner these people secure for their families, with but
little trouble, the most abundant supply of bacon. The
corn, which furnishes the most of their bread, is raised
with but little labor. After it is planted it is plowed
or cultivated, and "laid by" without any hoeing at all.
If they have enough to feed their hogs a short time before killing them, they do not gather this, but turn the
hogs into the corn-fields, and let them help themselves.
The drought that caused the famine in Kansas, in the
early history of that State, extended over this region.
As the breadth of ground planted here was so much
greater, the results were not so sad. But there was a
scarcity of corn such as the people had never known before. The price advanced from twenty and twenty-five
cents a bushel to a dollar and upward, and many were
unable to procure enough to make bread for their families. But the "mast" was abundant that fall, and
there was no lack of bacon. I visited many families
that lived almost entirely on meat. During the winter
I met a physician who told me that in his ride among
the hills he found whole families afflicted with a disease
that was entirely new in his experience. Upon consulting his books, he found it was scurvy, the result of living upon little besides bacon.

With this usually abundant supply of food, which
on account of the bad roads and the distance from market has but little pecuniary value; with houses and accommodations such as I have described; with but few

books, newspapers, and other kinds of reading; with a dearth of the excitements and amusements of the outside world, it is not so strange or wonderful that they are eager for pleasures and enjoyments that involve these displays of hospitality.

I know that my statements often appear incredible to many of my readers. But I trust that, after these "explanatory words," I shall not tax too largely either the faith of my readers or my own character for veracity.

CHAPTER VI.

THE BAPTISM OF A SCOTCH BABY IN THE WILDS OF THE
SOUTHWEST.

I wish to give my readers the details of a very pleasant incident in my experiences, quite incidental to my special work. I visited a small county-seat village in a very rough, wild region, where I had been directed to call upon a Methodist gentleman, who would render me efficient and cheerful aid in the prosecution of my labors. I met with the reception that had been promised, and made arrangements to preach "on the next day, which was the Sabbath." As the agents of the American Bible Society are chosen from the different religious denominations, they very naturally asked me with what church I was connected. When told that I was a Presbyterian, the gentleman and his wife turned at once to each other, a smile of unusual joy overspreading their features, and the lady, who was the first to speak, said:

"Well, Mr. and Mrs. Dinwiddie will be gratified at last."

The conversation that followed, and other visits and

conversations in the neighborhood, fully explained their joy at seeing me. The gentleman and lady alluded to were Scotch Presbyterians, who had been in this country but a few years, and they were very anxious to have their first-born child baptized by a minister of their own church. They, and a venerable man eighty-four years old, who had recently come from a distant part of the State to spend his declining years in the family of a widowed daughter, were the only persons in the county connected with that church, and they knew not when they might be favored with a visit from one of their own ministers. But, judging from the past history of the county, their prospects were dark indeed. A venerated father in this church, who was alive at the time of my visit, but has since gone to his reward, had preached in this county more than thirty years before on one of his missionary excursions through the State. I met those who had heard him preach and remembered his sermons. As far as could be ascertained, he was the last Presbyterian clergyman who had visited and preached in the county, and they knew not when to expect another. I subsequently saw this venerable preacher, and received from his own lips most interesting details of his explorations of these wild regions so many years before.

A week or two passed before I was able to visit this family, during which time I preached in rude log school-houses, in a ballroom, a court-house, from a "stand" erected for the purpose in the forest, and also standing

on *terra firma* at the foot of an oak-tree, the congregation being seated upon benches, or on the ground, under
the shade of surrounding oaks. In the different neighborhoods that I visited, I found the same general interest in behalf of this family and their child. According
to a Scottish custom, they would not call their child by
the name that had been chosen for it until that name
had been given to it in the sacred rite of baptism.
When asked by their neighbors the name of their child,
they would reply, " Oh, she has no name. She has not
been baptized yet. We call her ' Baby,' or some pet
name." This seemed very strange to the people, and
the dear little child that was growing up *without a name*
became the object of general sympathy and interest
throughout the county.

There is quite a celebrated watering-place (where my
mare won the two hundred and fifty dollars) some fifteen
miles from their forest home, and it was thought that
there might be some Presbyterian clergyman among the
visitors during the summer season, and a large number
of persons had promised this family that they would let
them know if any such clergyman arrived at the Springs,
that they might send for him to baptize their child.

As soon as I was able to do so, I set out to visit this
Scotch family, in whose history I had become very
deeply interested. A Christian brother, residing at the
county-seat and belonging to another denomination,
kindly consented to accompany me, and show me the

way to their residence. Our route was not over a road
that had been laid out by a compass, but was the most
of the way through the woods, winding its zigzag course
over hill, and valley, and stream, among the tall mon-
archs of the forest. It was a hot day in August, but the
dense foliage above us, as we rode through the "aisles of
the dim woods," protected us from the heat of the sun,
and our ride was altogether a pleasant one. After traveling some twelve or fifteen miles, we reached a "dead'-
ning," and soon were at the door of the log-cabin we
were seeking.

I will not attempt to describe the joy of that young
mother when my attendant introduced me to her as a
Presbyterian clergyman, and explained the object of our
visit. "Hope deferred maketh the heart sick, but when
the desire cometh it is a tree of life." Years had passed
since, a young and blooming bride, she had left the
heathery hills of Scotland for a home in our Western
wilds; but, until that moment, she had not seen a minister of the church of her home and her choice since the
day that her loved pastor had solemnized that rite in
which she gave herself to another, and sent her forth
with the warm blessings of a pastor's heart. The loneli-
ness of their forest home in a land of strangers was at
length cheered by the tiny echo of a new and welcome
voice in their rude dwelling. For many long months
the "joyful mother" had gazed upon the sweet face of
her lovely child, and longed, with unutterable longings,

to dedicate her first-born to God in his own appointed ordinance. As the months rolled on and swelled to years, the many friends of her home in Scotland mingled their sympathies with hers; and the pastor, who could not forget the lamb that had thus gone forth from his flock, expressed his strong desire to stretch his arms across the broad Atlantic, and baptize this child of the forest into the name of the Father, and of the Son, and of the Holy Ghost. At the time of our arrival the husband and father was absent from his house, attending to his flocks. He was a shepherd, and had selected his home here because for a small sum he could purchase a large tract of land over which his flocks might range. As his wife did not know in what direction he had gone, and he could not easily be found, we determined to wait until he should return.

In the mean time we learned that the young mother we had found in the wilds of the Southwest was born in the East Indies, and had been sent to Scotland when eight years old to be educated among her relatives. We listened to the story of the religious privileges they had enjoyed at home; heard of the old pastor who, for more than fifty years, had watched over the same flock, a volume of whose sermons and sacramental addresses made a part of their library, and learned to love the youthful colleague and subsequent pastor. We were shown what was at the same time a certificate of marriage and church-membership, certifying that "William D——

and Mary R—— were lawfully married on ——, and that they immediately thereafter started for America. They were then both in full communion with the Church of Scotland, and entitled to all church privileges." We were also shown that most appropriate of bridal gifts from a pastor—a beautiful Bible, presented as a parting gift to "Mrs. William D——, with best wishes for the temporal and spiritual welfare of herself and her husband. II Chronicles, xv, 2; Psalms, cxxxix, 1–12." How strikingly appropriate these references!

At length the father returned, and added his warm welcome and greeting to that we had already received from the mother. They had both evidently received that thorough religious training so peculiar to their nation, and here, far away from their native heath, in their wild forest home, it was exerting its influence, not only upon them, but upon many around them. That very morning a neighbor had sent them word that a Presbyterian clergyman (the writer) had preached at the Springs a few days before, and at once a younger brother was dispatched with a large farm-wagon, their only conveyance, to bring the stranger to their home, that he might baptize their child. Our route in going, and his in coming for me, were the same, but we failed to meet each other on account of the numerous tracks through the woods. On reaching the county-seat from which we had started in the morning, he learned that, to the joy of the neighborhood, we had already left for the purpose of baptizing the child. He immediately turned back, hastened home, and reached there soon after the arrival of his brother. A neighbor, an old acquaintance from their home in Scotland, and a family domestic, now made our number just that of those to whom Noah, that "preacher of righteousness," undoubtedly ministered after they entered the ark.

The necessary preparations for the baptism were soon made. In the center of that low-roofed cabin a cloth of snowy whiteness was spread upon a table, upon which a bowl of water was placed. That little company then arose, and reverently stood while, after a brief address to the parents, the simple, solemn ordinance of baptism was administered, and parents, child, and friends far away, were commended in prayer to a "covenant-keeping" God. The sacred stillness of that calm evening hour, the associations of a home far away, and the tender memories of the instructions of other years that clustered around these strangers, rendered the simple service most impressive, and pervaded all with solemn awe. We could but feel that he who had said to Abraham, "I will be a God to thee, and to thy seed after thee, in their generations, forever," had "bowed the heavens and come down"; and that he would ratify in heaven what had now been done on earth in the name of the Sacred Trinity. The happy mother pressed her fair-faced, beautiful child to her bosom with unwonted joy, and never did the sweet name Mary sound sweeter than when, with maternal fondness, she gazed into its clear blue eyes, and again and again, with alternate kisses, called her "Sweet Mary," "My Mary."

This was my first baptism; and the privilege of administering this Heaven-ordained rite, in circumstances like these, was compensation for months and years of such toils as they must endure who labor amid the moral desolations of our Western wilds.

CHAPTER VII.

BARBECUES; AND A BARBECUE WEDDING-FEAST IN THE SOUTHWEST.

THE barbecue was an established institution in the Southwest. It had in no other part of the country so many devotees. There was a charm in the name that would at any time call together a large concourse of people, on the shortest notice, and for any occasion. And the savory smell of roasted ox, sheep, shoats, turkeys, rabbits, or whatever else was prepared to appease the appetite of a crowd, would keep them together to hear the longest political speeches, listen to the most protracted school examinations, give their attention to the most elaborate expositions of the importance of some projected turnpike or railroad, and secure a patient waiting and an unbroken audience on any occasion when the *barbecue feast* was to be the agreeable conclusion.

I have a most distinct and vivid recollection of my first view of the process of barbecuing a whole ox. At the close of a long, hot day's ride, I had stopped to spend the night at a small and very inferior country tavern. On the opposite side of the road, immediately in front of it, there was a large forest. As I took my accustomed walk to the stable, to see that my horse was properly fed and cared for, before retiring for the night, I was attracted by the glimmerings of a fire among the tall, large forest-trees in the distance; and then I saw through the darkness the dusky forms of negroes moving among the trees, and hovering around some strangely concealed fire, only the gleams of which I could see. Ordinarily such a light in the woods or at the roadside would not have attracted my attention. The sight was a matter of daily and nightly occurrence. But it was usually wagoners, or movers, or travelers of some kind, camping for the night and cooking their supper. A very large proportion of the people that one met traveling with their own teams in the Southwest were entirely independent of all hotels and houses of entertainment. They had a long, narrow box attached to the hind end of their wagons, that served as a manger in which to feed their horses. When night overtook them, they hitched and fed their horses in the rear of their wagons. They then lighted a fire, and needed little besides a frying-pan and coffee-pot to prepare a supper of bacon, corn-dodgers, and coffee, to which hunger and good digestion gave a relish such as pampered and sated epicures never know. Almost invariably their wagons were covered with coarse brown duck-cloth or canvas, which was stretched over hoops, and, if not provided with tents, they made their beds under this covering. Wagoners who transported goods, flour, and other commodities long distances, as well as movers and others, usually traveled in company, so that whenever they camped for the night, which they usually aimed to do near some spring or brook, they presented a very picturesque and animated scene. The view which attracted my attention had none of these accessories and surroundings, and I strolled into the woods to see what it might be. On arriving at the spot my curiosity was abundantly gratified and rewarded. I saw for the first time an immense ox in the process of being barbecued. And this was the process: A large trench had been dug in the ground, about six or seven feet wide, eight or ten feet long, and four or five feet deep. This trench had been filled with the best quality of beech or maple wood from the body of the trees. This had been set on fire and burned until there was left a bed of burning coals, some two or three feet deep, that did not emit a particle of smoke. The slaughtered ox had been laid completely open, and two large spits, about eight feet long, had been thrust through each fore and hind leg lengthwise, and four negroes or more, taking hold of the ends of these spits, had laid the ox over this trench above this bed of burning coals. There the bovine monarch lay, cooking as beautifully as in my childhood I had seen many a turkey, suspended by a long string, swinging before the large wood-fire that was burning and

blazing upon the ample hearth of our family kitchen.
And it was upon the same principle—the juices were
all cooked in. The negroes were gathered around the
ox, with large swabs upon long sticks, with which they
incessantly "basted" it, with a liquid prepared for
this purpose and standing in large kettles on either
side of the trench. From time to time the large bed
of coals was stirred, and occasionally they performed
the difficult feat of turning over the entire ox, so
that each side might be cooked at an equal rate of
progress. This work they greatly enjoyed. There was
enough of the wild and strange about it to gratify
their excitable natures. For the time being they were
supremely happy. The stillness of the night, the
surrounding darkness, and the gleams of that large and
brightly burning bed of coals in the overhanging tree-tops,
gave to the whole scene a weird character which awoke
all the enthusiasm of their untutored natures. Through
the long night they cheerfully plied their task, stirring
up from the depths the live burning coals, and "basting"
and turning the ox as often as was necessary. Frequently they sang those strange, wild African songs that they
are accustomed to improvise while at work and upon
all kinds of occasions, and as they echoed among the
forest-trees and floated out upon the night-air, the soft,
sweet melody was most enchanting. As I left to go to
my room for the night, and turned to look back upon
them from the darkness, the strange scene seemed not

5

unlike a company of Druid priests offering a sacrificial victim in some grand old English forest. In the morning I made them another visit. Many of the coals had turned to ashes, and the bed was much reduced in depth. But when the negroes put in their long poles, they stirred up an abundance of bright coals from the bottom. The ox, which had been placed over the fire at sundown the night before, was to be cooked until noon, when the grand barbecue dinner was to be eaten. The smaller animals, such as sheep and shoats and the various kinds of poultry, were to be placed over the fire in time to be nicely cooked by this hour. At that time every portion of the ox would be thoroughly done to the bone; not baked and burned and dried, but made more juicy and tender and sweet than any one has ever once dreamed that the best of beef could be who has not eaten it cooked in this manner. I have never, at the most magnificent hotels, or the most luxurious private tables, eaten any kind of meat, poultry, or game that was so rich, tender, and agreeable to the taste as that barbecued in the manner I have described.

This was a political barbecue, at which several distinguished speakers, candidates for various offices, were to address the people. But my engagements for preaching, and other duties connected with my mission the next day, were such that I was compelled to leave immediately after breakfast. I could not hear the speeches, see the long tables, made of rough boards, spread under the forest-trees, participate with the immense throng in their barbecue dinner, and witness and enjoy all the strange and varied scenes and incidents inseparably connected with such a gathering of all the "sovereigns" in the Brush. But what I have said will suffice to give my readers the *modus operandi* of a barbecue. It will be seen that it is the simplest possible manner of preparing a dinner for a large concourse of people. It requires neither building, stove, oven, range, nor baking-pans. It involves no house-cleaning after the feast. It soils and spoils no carpets or furniture. And in the mild, bountiful region where the ox and all that is eaten are raised with so little care, the cost of feeding hundreds, or even thousands, in this manner is merely nominal. Hence barbecues have been for a long time so common and popular in the Southwest. There have been unnumbered political barbecues, where the eloquence peculiar to that region has been developed, and where vast audiences have been moved by its power, as the trees beneath which they were gathered have been swayed by the winds. In the published life and speeches of Henry Clay are several that were delivered at different barbecues, where he addressed the people on state and national affairs, with an eloquence and power equal to, if not greater than, that with which he enchained the Senate. There have been barbecues in connection with school-examinations, and Sabbath-school celebrations where educational and religious topics have been discussed. There have been barbecues in connection with meetings in favor of turnpikes, railroads, and all kinds of internal improvements. There have been uncounted barbecue-dances, and barbecues for more occasions than I can name. But of all these I will only describe a large wedding, that was succeeded by a barbecue-supper, that I had the pleasure of attending.

I had spent the Sabbath at a small county-seat village, and on Monday morning my kind friend and hostess said to me: "We are to have a large wedding on Thursday night of this week, and, if possible, you must stay in the county long enough to attend it. Mr. C——'s only daughter is to be married to Mr. R——, our county clerk, and, as Mr. C—— is a widower, I leave home this morning to go and assist them in their preparations."

As I was obliged to visit several persons in different parts of the county, on business connected with my Bible work, I planned my rides so as to reach the neighborhood in which Mr. C—— resided on the day appointed for the wedding. I received a cordial welcome from my lady friend, who was installed as presiding mistress for the occasion, and from the father of the bride, to whom she introduced me. He was an old and highly esteemed citizen of the county, and a warm personal and political friend of her husband..

It was on account of these relations between the families, and purely as an act of neighborly kindness, that she had left her own home to take charge of his family, and direct his servants during this, to them, eventful week. He belonged to the dominant party, and had represented his fellow-citizens in the Legislature of the State. Tall in stature, plainly dressed, mostly in home-made jeans, of simple, unstudied manners, his kind face and warm heart bespoke a man to be revered and loved by his neighbors and by all to whom he was known. He was in comfortable but not affluent circumstances—in the vernacular of the region, "a good liver." His house was of the prevailing style of architecture for the better class of plantation-houses in the Southwest and South. It was a two-story frame, with a wide hall or "passage" through the middle of it, and a chimney on each end, built outside of the house. In the rear, and communicating with it, was a log building, which had probably been the home of his early married life, in which the supper-table was to be spread for this occasion. Early in the afternoon the guests began to arrive. A few from adjoining counties, and from the greatest distance, persons of wealth and high social position, came in carriages; but by far the greatest number, both of ladies and gentlemen, arrived on horseback. The ladies almost invariably had a carpet-bag or sachel hung on the horn of their saddles, in which they brought the dresses in which they were to grace the occasion. A horseback-ride over such roads, and through such mud and clay as most of them had come, would not leave the most becoming wedding attire in a very presentable condition. Hence these arrangements to "dress" after their arrival. As they rode up, many of them with calico sunbonnets and butternut-colored riding-dresses, such as I have elsewhere described, and bespattered with mud, they looked more like bands of wandering gypsies than wedding guests. But the best of colored waiting-maids, from near and remote plantations, were in attendance, who took charge of the sachels, and of their young misses, and conducted them to some capacious dressing-room. Here each maid was anxious that her young "missus" should eclipse all the others, and under the manipulations of these ambitious servants they emerged from the room transformed, if not to wood-nymphs and fairies, at least to a becomingly attired and very bright and happy throng.

It was often very interesting to me to witness the solicitude and pride of these family servants in the appearance made and the attentions received by their young mistresses, and the art which they frequently displayed in aiding or defeating matrimonial alliances that were agreeable or otherwise to them. This was often a very important matter to them, as it involved the question whether they were to have a kind or an unkind master. If the suitor pleased them, they poured into his ears the most extravagant praises of their young "missus," and waited upon him with the most marked attention and delight. But if they knew that his temper and habits were bad, and thought he would make an unkind master, they did not fail to repeat, in ears where it would be most effective, all that they knew to his discredit. In this manner they have aided in making and defeating many matches.

As the sun declined, the arrivals increased until the numbers swelled to scores, to fifties, and, when all had assembled, there were in and around the house more than two hundred. It was a genial, happy throng. All were in the best possible humor. There were pleasant, kindly greetings between the old, and frolic and flirtations among the young. At about nine o'clock the wedding ceremony was announced, and as many of the guests as possible assembled in the largest room. The bride and groom, with bridesmaids and groomsmen becomingly attired, entered the room where we were gathered, and the ceremony was performed by a clergyman of the neighborhood, which was followed by the usual congratulations and greetings.

But there had been barbecuing and cooking of all kinds for days before, and very soon we followed the bride and groom with our ladies to the supper-room. The tables were arranged diagonally across the room from corner to corner, in the form of the letter X, so as to accommodate the largest number. There was the greatest abundance of barbecued meats, and poultry of different kinds, with a variety of cakes, pies, and everything else to make a hearty and bountiful feast. This was enjoyed with the keenest relish by all those who had gained admittance to the supper-room; and, when their appetites were fully satisfied, they retired to give place to others. These in turn gave place to others, and so tableful succeeded tableful for hours. While the feasting was going on, the others were en- joying themselves in conversation and general hilarity. Not a few occupied the large porch, and enjoyed a smoke and social chat. I sat down here and had a long talk with the father of the bride. He told me that, after inviting his particular friends, legislators, mem- bers of the bar, and others, from adjoining counties and distant neighborhoods, he had put a negro boy upon a horse and directed him to go to every family, rich and poor, within a circle of a few miles around his home, and invite them all to the wedding. I think that very few that could possibly get there had remained at home. It was a thoroughly promiscuous crowd. It embraced all ages and all grades of people that the region pro- duced, and all seemed equally to enjoy the gathering, as they were free to do in their own way. Some time after midnight I gratified my curiosity by going into the supper-room and asking my lady friend, who was the mistress of ceremonies, if she had any idea how many persons had already taken supper. She replied :

"I had not thought of that, but I can easily tell. The table has been set each time with thirty-two plates, and this is the fifth tableful."

And still others were waiting, and after them all the colored servants were to have their feast—in all, more than two hundred.

Later in the night a gentleman residing in the neighborhood invited me and several other gentlemen to go home and lodge with him. Before leaving, my lady friend came to me, and said :

"You must come back here and get your breakfast in the morning."

I replied :

"Is it possible that you will have anything to eat after feeding this great crowd ?"

"Oh, yes," said she, opening a door, and directing me to look into a room where the provisions were stored; "we have five barbecued shoats that have not been touched yet."

We mounted our horses, and rode through the darkness to my lodging-place for the night. Beds were soon divided and scattered over the floor, making pallets enough for each of us. The wife of my hospitable friend, with the most of the ladies in attendance, remained at the house and slept in this same manner, covering the floors of the different rooms. Husbands and wives were generally separated that night, the gentlemen going to the different houses in the neighborhood to sleep, as we had done. When we arose in the morning, my host said:

"We shall all have to go back to get our breakfast. There is not a knife, fork, or dish in the house. They are all at the wedding."

This was the condition of most of the houses in the neighborhood. When we returned, we found a large company and an abundant breakfast. After mingling with the departing guests for a time, I renewed my congratulations and good wishes for the happy pair, and bade good-by to my kind friends, greatly pleased with this entirely new experience at a wedding.

Such is a simple, unadorned narrative of a wedding, with its barbecue feast, at which I was a guest in the Southwest. How unlike those that I have attended in our largest cities! But who shall say at which there was the greatest and most universal happiness, whether where wealth and fashion held high carnival, or at this more simple and primitive gathering and feasting of old neighbors and friends in the Southwest?

CHAPTER VIII.

I HAVE never known such remarkable and pleasing results follow the reading of the Bible, without any human help, as among the ignorant people I have visited, living in wild and neglected regions in the Brush. I propose in this chapter to give a detailed account of the results that followed its presentation, by Mr. J. G. K——, to families living among the hills upon the head-waters of a stream that I thought was rightly named "Rough Creek." Mr. K—— was a venerable and faithful Bible-distributor, sixty-four years old, and he loved, above everything else, to go from house to house with the Word of God, and strive by simple, earnest exhortation and fervent prayer to lead souls to Christ. While prosecuting his labors in this neglected region, he found in one neighborhood sixteen families out of twenty without a Bible, and supplied the most of them by gift.

This region of country was exceedingly wild, broken, and inaccessible, there being no main public road leading to it. The hills were high and steep, the valleys narrow, and the people were scattered along the creeks and over the hill-sides, with no other roads leading to them than neighborhood paths. Mr. K—— told me that he never could have found all these families had not a young man who was born in the vicinity (who had since become a Methodist preacher) volunteered to accompany him as a guide. He had hunted deer, foxes, wildcats, and other game over these hills until he knew every locality and path. Entering these rude, humble cabins, they explained the nature of their work, supplied the families with the Word of God by sale or gift, and then, after kindly and earnestly urging upon them the worth of the soul and the importance of securing at once an interest in Christ, they bowed with them in prayer, and humbly and earnestly besought God's blessing upon them. There was a strange interest in these visits. The voice of prayer had never before been heard in many of these dwellings. Though their visits were so strange and unusual in their nature, they were everywhere kindly received, the mild, benignant face of the venerable distributor making him everywhere a welcome visitor. Where will not a face full of geniality and sunshine secure a welcome for its possessor?

As he was concluding his prayer at one of these cabins, the old man, who had been absent, returned, and hearing the strange sound in his house, cried out, in astonishment, "*Wake, snakes!*" But, on going into the house when the prayer was concluded, our visitor received him with a smile, explained to him the nature of his visit, and at once made a personal religious appeal to him. The old man treated his visitor very kindly, though he seemed to be in a very jocular mood, and replied to most of his remarks with some playful speech. But when his visitor left he went out with him, and assisted him in getting on to his horse, and invited him to call again whenever he should pass that way. But generally their exhortations were listened to with deep solemnity and awe, and their visits evidently made a deep religious impression upon the neighborhood.

Not many weeks after these visits of Mr. K——, reports were received that several persons in this neighborhood had been hopefully converted; and for a year or more I was almost constantly hearing from various sources of the wonderful work of grace that was going on there. The statements in regard to the number and character of the conversions were so remarkable that I was unwilling to make them public until I had made a personal visit to the neighborhood, and seen with my own eyes what God had wrought. I subsequently made that visit, and can truly say that the half had not been told me. My powers are not equal to the work of giving an adequate description of the great change that had been wrought through the power of God's Word and Spirit, but I will give some of the main facts.

I arrived at a house to which I had been directed,

near this neighborhood, about midday, having traveled for miles in the foot-paths that led from one cabin to that of the next neighbor. Where the path was blind and difficult to follow, the people would often send a little boy or girl along to show me the way. On making myself known as a preacher, and the agent of the American Bible Society, I was at once greeted with the usual question, "Won't you preach for us to-night?"

I gladly assented, as I had made the journey to learn the real condition of things, and I was anxious to see as many of the people as possible. Word was at once sent over the hills in different directions that I would preach that night in a log-house that had been erected since the visit of Mr. K—— for a school and meeting house; and shell-bark-hickory torches were at once prepared to light me and the hospitable family that entertained me to and from the place of meeting. This house was upon a hill in the midst of the woods, and at some distance from any clearing, having been placed there on account of its central position in the neighborhood. Though the notice was short, and the night dark, and all who came had to make their way by torchlight through the forest, the house was well filled, and it was a real pleasure to unfold and enforce the truths of the Gospel, in simple language, to a group whose solemn stillness and attention showed that they listened indeed as to a message from Heaven.

At the close of our services it was a rare and beautiful sight to see the audience disperse from that rude sanctuary, some on foot, and some on horseback —a father, mother, and three children upon a single horse — the oldest child in front of the father, the second behind the mother, and the third in the mother's arms, their flaming torches lighting up the grand old forest, as they set out for their homes with parting words of Christian hope and cheer.

In the prosecution of my inquiries I learned that the first person who had been converted in the neighborhood, after the visit of Mr. K——, was Mr. Jake G——, who had received a Testament in the following manner. When Mr. K—— and his guide were making their visits, they called at a house where there were eight children, and the parents were both gone from home. On inquiring of the children if their parents had a Bible, they said they did not know— meaning, undoubtedly, that they did not know what a Bible was.

Without dismounting, they gave the children a Testament, and told them to give it to their parents when they came home.

Not long after this the guide who accompanied Mr. K—— met the man at whose house they had left the Testament, and he immediately said: "I'm mighty sorry I was not at home when you and old man K—— were around with them books, for I'm mightily

pleased with the little book you left at my house.
Joe H—— told me you had some bigger ones" (Bibles) " at his house, and if I had been at home I
would have got one of them bigger ones sure; for
I'm mightily pleased with the little one. I can't read,
and my wife and children can't read; but Brother
Joe's wife can read, and she comes over to our house,
and we get her to read out of that little book; and
it's mighty pretty reading. I've heard reading afore,
but I never heard any reading afore that I wanted
to hear read again. *But that little book I do take to
mightily.* Brother Fred's wife can read, too, and we
get her to read out of the little book; and everybody
that comes to our house that can read, we get them to
read out of that little book; and—*I don't know what
it is* — I never heard any such reading afore; *every
time they read to me out of that little book it makes
me cry, and I can't help it.*"

I have already said that this man was the first
person who was converted in the neighborhood after
the visit of the Bible-distributor. They read "*that
little book*" until he and his wife, and those two brothers
and their wives, became savingly acquainted with its
truths, and they, with many others in the neighborhood,
became the humble and devoted followers of Christ. I
learned that this Mr. Jake G——, who had received and
who now loved his "little book," as I have described,
belonged to a family remarkable for their ignorance and

irreligion. Though he had eight children, his grand-
father was yet alive, more than ninety years old, and
still a very hardened sinner. He had come to this neighborhood from southwestern Virginia more than thirty
years before. He had had eighteen children, thirteen of
whom lived to marry, and nine of whom were settled
immediately around him. None of his children could
read a word except two of the youngest, who had attended school a little after leaving Virginia, and, though
all of them had large families, all of them were without
the Bible *but two*. One son and one daughter had married persons who had a Bible. The two Bibles that had
been obtained by marriage were the only Bibles in this
large family connection when Mr. K—— visited the
neighborhood and supplied them all.

The father of the man who had received the Testament was sixty-two years old; had reared a family of
nine children, not one of whom nor himself could read,
and all of them had grown up and married but two; and
that large family had never owned a Bible. The mother
could read, and Mr. K—— gave her a Bible. *Now she
and her husband and six of their children* were numbered with the people of God, and though unable to read
were humble learners at the feet of Jesus.

The morning after my sermon, accompanied by a
small boy, whom my host kindly sent along as a
guide, I rode through the woods and over the hills to the
house of Mr. Jake G——, where, several months before,

the "little book" had been left by the Bible-distributor
and his guide.   He was among my hearers the night before, and I had sought an introduction to him, had a
short conversation with him, and told him I would come
and see him in the morning.   I was particularly anxious
to spend a few hours with him in his own home, and get
the story of the great change that had been wrought in
himself and in the neighborhood, from his own lips, and
in his own genuine Brush vernacular.

There is to me a strange interest and pleasure in
hearing one whose soul has been thoroughly subdued by
the power and grace of God, who as yet knows little of
the Bible, and less of the set phrases in which religious
thoughts are usually communicated, give expression
to the warm and glowing emotions of his soul, in language all his own.   There is often in these recitals the
highest type of simple, natural eloquence in the singu-
larity, the quaintness, and the power of the language
used.

As I rode up the hill-side and hitched my horse to
the rail-fence in front of his log-cabin, he came out to
meet and welcome me.   But there was not that warmth
of cordiality with which he had shaken my hand the
night before.   As I entered the house with him and
took a seat, he remained standing, and walked about the
floor continually, with an uneasy, troubled air.   He was
a very tall man, was barefooted, and his only dress was a
shirt and pantaloons.   After some little conversation, he

turned to me and said, "How much does that little book sell for?"

I could not imagine why he asked the question, but replied at once, "Only a dime, sir." (The Bibles and Testaments were sold as near the cost - price in New York as possible, but as no pennies were used in any business transactions in all this region, we were obliged to sell this Testament, costing six and a fourth cents, for a dime.)

He did not make any response to my answer, but, after some further conversation, which I tried to keep up, he came and stood directly over me, and said, in a very sad tone of voice, "Well, sir, I have only got half enough to pay for that little book, but if I had the money I'd pay five dollars before I'd give it up."

Understanding at once that he supposed I was on a collecting tour, and that this was the cause of my visit and all his trouble, I said, "Why, sir, did you suppose I had come to get the pay for your little Testament?"

"H'ain't you?" asked his wife eagerly, a slight smile of hope passing over her earnest, expressive face.

"Why, no, indeed," said I; "that book was given to you. The Bible Society gives away a great many Bibles and Testaments, and all they want is to know that people make good use of them."

"Well, I declare!" said she, her face all radiant with joy. "We've been right smartly troubled about it all the morning. I knew we hadn't got money enough to pay for it, and I didn't know what we *should* do. I wouldn't give it up for nothing. I know none of us can't read any, but we get it read a mighty heap. I love to have it in the house, whether we can read or not. *That's the little book we're trying to go by now,* and whenever they gets together the first thing is to get out the little book, and it seems like they never get tired of it."

That was one of the most moving and beautiful tributes of affection and love for the Word of God to which I have ever listened. I see her now through the lapse of years, her bright, black eyes and her face all aglow with joy, as she sat at one side of her fireplace in that comfortless cabin. The chimney, made of sticks and mud, and standing on the outside of the house, had leaned away from the opening that had been cut through the logs for the fireplace, and left a large open space through which and the logs the winds blew upon her back about as freely as through a rail-fence. Where the brick or stone hearth should have been, there was only a bed of ashes and a few smoldering fire-brands. Two beds on one side of the room and a few rough articles of household furniture numbered all the comforts of their one apartment. Such were her surroundings, and yet I had made her one of the happiest mortals I have ever seen. As I looked into her black, expressive eyes and her bright face, which must have been beautiful in earlier years, it was hard to believe that she could not read a word—that she had never learned a single letter of the alphabet of her mother-tongue.

"Well," said an old man, who thus far had sat quite mute, "I'm sure my old woman makes good use of hers; she reads it about half the time. I believe she would go crazy if you should take her Bible away."

This old man, with his hair hanging down to his shoulders, his powder - horn, pouch, and other hunting equipments hanging at his side, had entered the house with his gun in hand just as I rode up, having apparently just returned from a morning hunt. I now learned that he was the father of the man at whose house I was —the man in whose family so great a change had been wrought since Mr. K—— had given his wife the Bible. After I had satisfied them that they were not to lose their Testament and Bible, all tongues were unloosed, and I wish it were in my power to give in detail the conversation that followed.

"Can't you stay and preach for us to-night?" said the old man. "We can send word around, and you'll have a house full. I want to hear you mightily. We didn't sleep any last night, hardly. Jake came home from meeting so full, and he was trying to tell us about the sermon. You ought to stay and see the G——s; you ought to hear them sing and pray."

I consented to preach again most gladly, and after full consultation among themselves as to whose house in the neighborhood would hold the most people, and arrangements had been made for circulating the notice, they all sat down and listened intently while I read to them out of the " little book," explaining the portions read as I would attempt to explain them to an infant-class in a Sabbath-school. I remember that the great change wrought in themselves and their neighbors seemed an incomprehensible mystery to them. So, looking out of the open door of their cabin and down the hill-side, I pointed them to the tops of the large forest trees that were swaying to and fro in the wind, and said :

" You see all those trees in motion, but can not see anything moving them. And yet you know what it is. You know that it is the wind. You can not see it, but you can hear its sound."

I then opened their " little book " (for I had pre-ferred to read to them out of their own prized treasure, that they might be sure, after I was gone, that they had in their possession all that I had read and explained to them), and read to them the story of the conversation of Christ with Nicodemus, calling their special attention to the passage : " The wind bloweth where it listeth, and thou hearest the sound thereof, but canst not tell whence it cometh or whither it goeth. So is every one that is born of the Spirit."

This passage was apparently new, and made the whole matter wonderfully clear to them, affording them the most intense pleasure and satisfaction. So I read, and they listened to these simple comments, for an hour or more with expressions of the deepest interest, and would evidently have listened thus for hours. We then all bowed upon our knees, and, after I had prayed, Mr. Jake G——, at my request, offered a prayer, such as he offered daily as he assembled his children around that family altar; a prayer so broken, so humble, so sincere, as to move the stoutest heart. I wish I could give the whole of it; but I only remember the first sentence, "O Lord, we bow down to call on thy name as well as we know how."

I spent the rest of the day with the old man, visiting different families, and in his own, reading the Bible to them, praying with them, and listening to their simple details of the wonderful change that had been wrought among them. Their own statements in regard to the exceeding ignorance and irreligion of the community corroborated the accounts I heard of them in all the country around.

"I've known a heap of people," said the old man, as we left the house, and started off through the woods, "but I never did know as bad a set as the G——'s" (his own family). "Every one of my boys played the fiddle, and every one of my children had rather dance than eat the best meal that could be got. Every one of my boys played cards and gambled. Every one of them would go to horse-races and shooting-matches, and get drunk, and fight, and get into all kinds of scrapes. And my boy Dock—that ain't his name, but that's what we all call him—I do wish you could hear Dock pray now—my boy Dock used to get drunk and have fits [delirium tremens], and when he was gone to a shooting-match or a log-rolling, or any such place, I'd go to bed at night, but I couldn't go to sleep. I'd just lie and wait to hear him holler, and I've gone out many a night and brought him into the house out of-the most awful places. And Sundays—why, I didn't hear a sermon in fifteen years. Sundays my yard was filled with people who came from all around here, and jumped, and played marbles, and shot at a mark, and frolicked, all day long. And such a thing as a hime " (hymn), continued the old man, " singin' himes or prayin', why, there wa'n't no such thing in all the neighborhood. When they first began to hold meetings around, there wa'n't nobody to raise the tunes. Now they know a heap of himes, and sometimes Jake leads the meetin', and sometimes Dock, and you ought to hear them all sing and pray now."

So the old man talked on, giving his simple narrative of these and a great many other facts, until at length we came to a log-house. This was the place where I was to preach that night, the home of a brother—the old man that had shouted " *Wake, snakes!* " at hearing Mr. K—— pray. He had since died, and died unconverted, and the account that the old man gave of the death of this brother was most touching. As his case grew more and more hopeless, those of his children and relatives who had been converted felt the deepest interest for him, talked with him as well as they knew how, and prayed with him; but all apparently in vain.

"I watched him from day to day," said the old man, "until I saw there was no hope for him. I knew that he must die, and I knew that he was not prepared. I shook hands with him, bid him good-by, and turned away from him, and thought I had no time to lose. I determined to try and get religion at once, and be prepared for death."

When at length his family and friends had gathered around his bed to see him die, his youngest daughter, that had lately been converted, who was about eighteen years old, but could not read a letter, agonized at the thought of his leaving the world unprepared, rushed forward, knelt at his bedside, and gave vent to her emotions in a prayer such as is rarely offered. Those who heard it were most of them as illiterate as herself, and incompetent to describe it; but from their accounts the scene was solemn, and the effect overpowering to all except the dying man. As she arose from her knees, he opened his eyes, and said, faintly, "I never expected that [to hear a prayer] from one of my children," and in a few moments breathed his last. During my visit here I asked this young lady if she could read. She replied:

"Oh, no, sir; I was always too industrious to take time to learn to read." Her arms were colored to above her elbows, where she had had them in the dye-tub, preparing the "butternut-woolsey" for the family use.

6

From this place the old man took me to his own house. As we went up to the door, his wife stood with her back to us, washing dishes, and he rapped at the door. She turned her head so as to see us both, but did not move her body or say a word. He then said :

"Old woman, see here!" (pointing to me), "here is a man that has come to get your Bible."

Looking at me a moment, she responded :

"You talk too much," and resumed her work.

We then entered the house, and he informed his wife and daughter who I was and that I was to preach that night. After I had talked with them a while, it was proposed that I should again read and explain the Bible to them. At his son's house, as they had all been so wicked, I had read, among other portions, the account of the persecutions and the conversion of the Apostle Paul, and given them a simple sketch of his subsequent history, and then pointed out the parts of the "little book" that this man who had been so wicked had been inspired to write. This story was almost if not entirely new to them, and they were greatly interested in it. When the family were seated, and I was about to read to them, the old man said to me :

"Can't you read that again that you read up at Jake's? That about—that—that—that what do you call him ?"

"Paul," said I.

"Yes, Paul, Saul, Paul. Read that about Paul. If that don't hit the nail on the head better than anything I ever heard afore!"

I, of course, consented, and went over the story again for the benefit of his family, and the facts seemed to lose none of their interest to the old man by their repetition. Having spent all the time desirable in reading and praying with this family, there were still a few hours before the preaching service began. Shall I introduce my readers more fully to this home in the Brush, and tell them how this time was passed? The house contained but a single room. The daughter of whom I have spoken was about eighteen or twenty years old, tall and large, wore a butternut-colored woolsey dress that she had probably spun and woven, and was barefooted. I had not been long in the house before she retired from their only room, in which I sat, and in honor of my arrival reappeared in another dress. I do not know where she made her toilet, only that it was the same ample and magnificent dressing-room first used by Mother Eve. The material of the dress in which she appeared was old-fashioned cheap curtain calico, with waving stripes some two or three inches wide running its entire length. Preferring perfect freedom and the comfort of the cooling breezes to considerations that would have been influential with most of my lady readers, in thus making her toilet she had chosen to remain stockingless and shoeless. A massive head of dark-brown hair, cut squarely off and pushed behind her ears, hung loosely down her neck.

When the dishes were washed and all the after-dinner work accomplished, and she was prepared to sit down and enjoy the conversation, she took from the rude mantle-tree above the fireplace a cob-pipe, and filled it with home-grown and home-cured tobacco from an abundant supply in a large pocket in her dress. Lighting her pipe, she took a seat at the right of her father, while I occupied a chair on his left. Soon large columns of smoke began to rise and roll away above her head as gracefully as I have ever seen them float around the head of the most fashionable smoker with the most costly meerschaum. Bending her right arm so that she could clasp the long stem of her pipe with her fore-finger, she rested the elbow in the palm of her left hand. Then, placing her right limb across her left knee, she swung the pendent foot slowly, as if in meditative mood, and yielded herself to the full enjoy-ment of her pipe and our conversation. Her name I should have said was Barbara. She was of a quiet, taciturn disposition, and rarely said anything, except as she was appealed to on some matter by her proud and happy father.

I have met some people who were so ignorant in regard to rustic manufactures that they did not know what a "cob"-pipe was. For the sake of any that may be similarly uninformed, I will describe one. It is made by taking a section of a common corn-cob some two or three inches in length, and boring or burning out with a hot iron the pith of the cob some two thirds of its length, and then boring or burning a small hole transversely through the cob to the base of the bowl already made, and inserting in this a small hollow reed or cane for a stem. These pipe-stems are long or short, from a few inches to two or three feet, according to the preference of those who are to use them. I have often been told by old smokers that no pipe was as pleasant or sweet as a cob-pipe. The great objection to them is that they have to be renewed so frequently.

Seated as I have already described, the hours passed away to the evident satisfaction of my entertainers. It is not an easy matter to maintain a conversation for several hours with those who have never read a word of their mother-tongue. Their stock of ideas is necessarily rather limited. But a very large experience in mingling with this class of people had given me such facilities that I was evidently already installed as a favorite in the family. I asked a great many questions in regard to the children and grandchildren, which were answered with the interest which always pertains to these inquiries. At length the old man returned the compliment by inquiring very particularly into my own family affairs. When pressed upon this subject, as I almost universally was by families in the Brush, I was compelled to tell them that my family was very small—as small as possible

—just that of the Apostle Paul; in plain language, that I was that quite unusual character, a clerical bachelor. The old man was astonished. I think he was gratified. His face glowed with some new emotion. He was evidently willing on our short acquaintance to receive me as a son-in-law. Turning his pleased, animated face to me, and leaning forward in his chair, he lifted his right hand, and, pointing with an emphatic gesture to his daughter, said:

"Well, preacher, my gals is all married but Barbara here, and she is ready, sir."

Miss Barbara retained her hold upon the long stem of her cob-pipe, and smoked on, wellnigh imperturbable at this sudden culmination of affairs, though I think that, like myself, she was somewhat startled and moved, for I could see an evident increase in the swinging movement of her still pendent right foot.

But I must pass over other and interesting incidents of the day. Night came, and with it the congregation that had been promised. Temporary seats had been provided, and the log-cabin was closely packed. As the last of the company were arriving, it began to sprinkle, and as our services progressed the rain fell in torrents. There was grandeur in the storm as the wind howled among the trees and the rain beat upon the roof but a few feet above our heads. As the most of the company could not read, and all were very ignorant, my sermon was as simple as I could possi-

"Well, Preacher, my gals is all married but Barbara here,
and she is ready, sir."

bly make it. It was listened to with an eager interest, reminding me of the words of the prophet: "Thy words were found, and I did eat them; and thy word was unto me the joy and rejoicing of my heart." Those simple babes in Christ had as yet no idea of a meeting without special efforts for the conversion of the impenitent; and, in response to my appeal made after the sermon, a little girl, some twelve or fourteen years old, came forward to be prayed for. As she started, the audience were greatly moved. She was the great-grandchild of the hoary-headed and hardened sinner who had raised his large family as I have already described, and who still lived and looked on unmoved at the wonderful work God was doing among his children and his children's children. She was the eldest daughter of Dock G——, and after I had instructed her and pointed her to Christ as best I could in these circumstances, and several prayers had been offered for her, her father knelt by her side and poured forth the yearning desires of his burdened soul in her behalf. It was a prayer of confession of parental unfaithfulness, of thanksgiving for what God had already done, and of earnest, importunate wrestlings for one that was a part of himself and must live for ever. It was a prayer such as I had never heard before. I did not wonder that his father had said to me in the morning, "I do wish you could hear Dock pray now." Though he could not read, his mind was evidently of a superior order, and the language of his prayer was not such as he had acquired by hearing others pray, but was entirely his own. It was deeply affecting to hear such familiar thoughts, uttered in language so strange and unusual.

As the rain continued to pour in torrents and the night was fearfully dark, the meeting was continued to a late hour, and I was gratified in hearing them sing and pray a long time. Their hymns were mostly those that they had learned by hearing them sung by others, and their prayers were the simple, earnest utterances of those who seemed evidently to have been taught of God. At length the meeting closed, and though the rain still poured without abatement, and the night was fearfully dark, several of the company, who had left young children at home, started out in the storm to make their way home through the woods and across swollen streams by following, without torchlight, their winding neighborhood paths. But the most of the congregation remained until near midnight, when the rain abated and it became lighter. Others now started for home, some on foot and some on horseback, to find their way through the forest for two or three miles, up and down hills and across streams, where I had found it a difficult matter to make my way by daylight. With a number so large that I did not undertake to count them, I spent the night in their cabin, and received from the family the kindest treatment it was in their power to bestow.

First of all, at the close of the meeting, the cob,

clay, and all other pipes were brought out, and family and guests sat down to enjoy a social smoke and chat. Though I have spent so many years where tobacco is grown and almost universally used, though I have enjoyed the hospitality of a great many families where the mothers and daughters both chewed and "dipped," I have never learned to use the weed. Though I do not smoke, I have very often been most thoroughly smoked. In this company of social smokers, composed of old men and young men, old women and young women, I was more favored than I have often been in the most elegant apartments of the most magnificent dwellings. The fireplace, several feet long, filled with ashes, made an ample spittoon, and the large "stick" chimney, aided by the winds that circulated freely through the cabin, afforded what I have so often wished for—an ample funnel for the escape of the smoke and fumes of the tobacco. Uncultivated as this company was, it was evident that they were gifted with capacities for enjoying the weed equal to those of the most refined circles I have ever met.

Having smoked to their satisfaction, and the hour of midnight being passed, I was pointed to a bed in one corner of the room which I was to occupy. I had not been in it long before some bedfellow got in to share it with me. I soon discovered that it was my would-be father-in-law, and that he slept with his boots on—I suppose to save the trouble of drawing them off and on. How or where the rest of my congregation slept, I do not know, for, on getting into bed, I had turned my face to the log wall, and, being exceedingly wearied with the labors of the day and the night, I was soon oblivious to all around me, and lost in sleep. When I awoke in the morning, my friend, who had shared the bed with me, and who had evidently awaked some time before, greeted me with the friendly salutation :

" How dy, partner ? " his boots, at the moment, greeting my vision as they extended beyond our bed blankets or quilts.

After breakfast, I bade good-by to the kind friends whose rough but generous hospitality I had thus enjoyed, with many thanks on their part for my visit, with many regrets at my departure, and with repeated requests that I would visit and preach for them again. But my farewell here, as in thousands of other cases, was a final farewell. I was not to meet them again, except, as is so often sung, in one of their wild, favorite religious songs :

" When the general roll is called."

During this visit I learned that about a hundred persons had been converted in this neighborhood since the visit of the Bible-distributor. Among them were about thirty members of the family to which I have so often alluded, in which this good work had its com-

mencement in the reading of that little Testament.
There had formerly been no regular preaching in the immediate neighborhood, but a Cumberland Presbyterian
minister had preached once a month in a private house
not far from them. It was the house to which I had
been directed, and the family who had so kindly entertained me and circulated the appointment for my first
sermon in the neighborhood. The preacher was the
faithful man of God who had preached and officiated
in the marriage at the "basket-meeting in the Brush"
which I have already described. He had changed the
place of holding his meetings, and preached regularly
once a month in the new log-house in which I preached
on the night of my arrival. In addition to his regular
services, he had held protracted meetings, and his earnest and devoted labors had been greatly blessed in carrying forward this remarkable work of grace. Methodist
preachers had also visited the neighborhood at different times, and held meetings at which numbers had
been hopefully converted. All who had made a public profession of religion had united with these two
denominations, and there was the utmost peace and
harmony among them. The dark spirit of sectarian-
ism seemed as yet to have found no place among them,
and all who beheld them were compelled to say, as
should be said of all those of different names who profess to be the disciples of Christ, "Behold how these
brethren love one another."

At the time of my visit and for some months before, the only regular preaching in the neighborhood was that once a month by Mr. W——, the Cumberland Presbyterian minister. But they held a prayer-meeting which was conducted by themselves on all the other Sabbaths, and once during each week. At these meetings they read the Scriptures, and sang and prayed, and with tearful eyes and warm and glowing hearts rehearsed to their friends and neighbors the simple story of the love and grace of God as it had been manifested to them. To those who had been familiar with their former lives, there was a convincing, an almost resistless, power in their services, and they had often been owned of God in the salvation of souls. Many had been induced to come long distances to attend these meetings, and had gone away, saying, "Surely this is the work of God, for only his power could enable such people to offer such prayers." I was told that even the little children had caught the prevailing spirit, and had commenced a "play" that was entirely new in the neighborhood. When their parents were gone to night-meetings, as they often were, the little children who were left at home alone entertained themselves by playing "meeting"—going through with all the services as they had seen them at the meetings they had attended with their parents. I tried to learn of one mother— the one who was so grateful that she was not to lose her "little book"—what her children would say at these meetings, but she could only tell me of one little fellow four or five years old, that she pointed out to me, who would get up and very seriously repeat over and over the words, "Oh, them dear little children in heaven! them dear little children in heaven!"

I was very greatly interested in learning from the remarks that I heard in both this and the surrounding neighborhoods of the uniformity of sentiment in regard to the religious character of this work. In a long conversation with a man who had known these people from his boyhood, and whose Christian heart had been greatly rejoiced at what he had seen and heard, I said:

"There must be a very great change among them?"

"Indeed there is," said he, emphatically. "It's a smart miracle!"

Among all the persons of different classes that I saw, I met no one who seemed to doubt in the least that it was a genuine work of grace. "It is the Lord's doing, and it is marvelous in our eyes."

CHAPTER IX.

CANDIDATING; OR, OLD-TIME METHODS AND HUMORS OF
OFFICE-SEEKING IN THE SOUTHWEST.

I HAVE found no class of people in the Southwest so
omnipresent as office-seeking politicians. I have visited
no neighborhood so remote, no valley so deep, no mountain so high, that the secluded cabins had not been honored by the visits of aspiring politicians, eager to secure
the votes of their "sovereign" occupants. In multitudes of such cabins and settlements, their first impressions in regard to me were that I was either a sheriff,
collecting the county and State taxes, or a "candidate"
soliciting votes. The one vocation was as general and as
universally recognized as an honorable employment as
the other. If I did not make myself known as a clergyman as soon as I arrived at many of these out-of-the-
way cabins, I was frequently greeted with the salutation:

"How dy, sir? I reckon you are a candidate, stranger!"

Some months preceding each election these aspirants for official honors publicly announced themselves as candidates for the particular office that they sought. In those States where the election was held the first Monday in August, these announcements were usually made the preceding spring at the February county or circuit court. On such occasions the court adjourned for the afternoon, and after dinner the crowds in attendance gathered in the court-house, and, one after another, all the aspirants for all the different offices, State and national, came before the assembled people, announced themselves as candidates, and set forth their qualifications for the office sought and their claims upon the suffrages of their fellow-citizens. Sometimes half a dozen or more would announce themselves as candidates for the same office. In listening to their speeches one would be led to think that the chief excellence and glory of our Constitution was that it secured to every citizen the right to be an office-seeker. "My fellow-citizens, I claim the *right* of an American citizen to come before you and solicit your suffrages," was asserted by a great many of these candidates, and very often by those who could present but a sorry list of other claims for the office sought.

I have often found these gatherings occasions of the rarest interest and sport. On one occasion the candidate's name was *Coulter*, and the office sought was the county clerkship. The incumbent was a consumptive, in such poor health that he had been compelled to spend

the winter in a milder climate, and it was doubtful if
he would be able to discharge the duties of his office
another term. "My fellow-citizens," said Mr. Coulter,
"I am very sorry for Mr. Anderson [who was present],
our worthy county clerk, sorry that his health is so poor—
sorry that he was obliged to leave us last winter, and go
and breathe the balmy breezes of a more genial climate.
But as he was gone, and there was some doubt about his
coming back, I did not think it would be out of the way
to try my Coulter a little. I experimented with it. It
worked well. I tried it in several precincts. It ran
smooth and cut beautifully. I am so much pleased with
the way it works that I am determined to enter it for the
race." This play upon his name was received with great
favor. His old father sat upon a table immediately
under the judge's seat from which he spoke, and gazed
up at him with open mouth and the most intense parental pride and joy. The crowd cheered to the echo, and
I learned some months afterward that this remarkable
(?) display of wit was rewarded by the clerkship sought.

In these public speeches, and on all other occasions,
both public and private, this pursuit of office was always
spoken of as a "race." The most common remarks and
inquiries in regard to any political canvass were such
as these :

"I intend to make the 'race.'" "It will be a
very close 'race.'" "Do you think Jones will make the
'race?'" "Smith has a strong competitor, but I think

he will make the 'race.' " "I will bet you fifty dollars that Peters will make the 'race.' "

To "make the race" was to secure an election.

On another occasion, I heard a speaker who had been a candidate for the same office, and had canvassed his county, making speeches in every neighborhood, for twelve successive years. Though I saw him very often and knew him very well, I never heard him speak but once.

A part of his speech I could not forget. It was as follows:

"Fortunately or unfortunately, my fellow - citizens, some twelve years ago I was seized with a strong desire to represent my county in the lower house of the Legislature of my native State. Fellow-citizens, you all know me. I was raised among you. I was a poor boy. I am a poor man now. I ask you to vote for me as an encouragement to the poor boys of the county, that I may be an example to them—that they may point to me and say, 'There is a man, that was once as poor as any of us, who has been honored with a seat in the Legislature of his native State.' I have taught school a good many winters, and the boys that I have taught like me. They will give me their votes. I have sometimes thought I should have to teach school over the county until I had taught boys enough to elect me."

I can not go through with all of his speech, but his peroration was too rich to omit:

"My fellow-citizens, when I look back over the twelve years since I became a candidate for this office, I feel encouraged. When I look back and think of the very few that for years gave me any encouragement, and compare them with the numbers that now promise me their votes, I am proud of my success. I begin to feel that my hopes are about to be realized—that a majority of my fellow-citizens will honor me with their suffrages, and that I shall proudly go up to the Capitol and take my seat among the legislators of the State. But, fellow-citizens, if, unfortunately, I should fail in this election, *I take the present opportunity to announce myself as a candidate in the next race.*"

This candidate was like the suitor whom the lady accepted to get rid of him. Though a large number of his fellow-citizens were very intelligent men, they finally concluded not to vote against him, and allow him to be elected. I afterward saw him in the Legislature, and he was certainly superior to some of his colleagues. He introduced me to a fellow-member from the mountains who could not read or write at all; and told me, privately, that he read and answered all the letters that passed between him and his family and constituents. Mr. George D. Prentice was accustomed to give this legislator from the mountains an almost daily notice in the "Louisville Journal."

After these public announcements were made, the candidates entered upon their work in dead earnest.

They often issued printed handbills, announcing the days on which they would speak at different places. They traveled together, and addressed the same crowds in rotation. These political discussions between candidates for the higher offices, such as governor, member of Congress, etc., were often very able and eloquent. Indeed, I have rarely, if ever, heard more able political discussions than some of these. Where they canvassed a State or Congressional district together, they spoke in rotation, an hour each by the watch, and then concluded with half-hour speeches. This gave to each an opportunity to answer the arguments of the other. As both addressed the same audience, and each was applauded and cheered by his own party, they were both stimulated and excited to the highest degree possible. Each wished not only to gratify his political friends by the ability and skill with which he discussed the questions at issue, but to secure from the audience as many votes for himself as possible. They were like lawyers before a jury, each anxious to secure a verdict in his own favor. I have often thought that this method of conducting a political campaign had many advantages over that which generally prevails in the Northern and Eastern States, where a candidate, with no ability to speak, is nominated by a caucus, and the parties afterward meet in separate mass-meetings, and the speakers convince voters that are already convinced and annihilate opponents that are not there. In this manner neither party has the opportunity to correctly and fairly represent its views to the other.

But public political discussions made but a small part of the labor performed by the great majority of these candidates. They solicited the votes of the people in private, and on all sorts of occasions. Some of them mounted their horses, and went from house to house together as thoroughly as if they were taking the census. A story is told of two opposing candidates who spent a night together at a cabin. Each was anxious to secure the "female influence" of the family in his own favor, and one of them took the water-bucket and started for the distant spring to get a pail of water, thinking to make a favorable impression on the hostess by rendering her this aid in preparing the coffee for their supper. His opponent, not to be outdone by this master-stroke of policy, devoted himself to the baby with such success that he won its favor, and succeeded in getting it into his arms. The other candidate returned from his long walk with his well-filled water-bucket, to see his opponent bestowing the most affectionate caresses and kisses upon a baby that very sadly needed a thorough application of the water he had brought, and to hear him pour into the mother's charmed ear abundant and glowing words of praise for her hopeful child. The water-bucket was set down in despair. It is quite unnecessary to say which of the candidates secured the vote from that cabin.

These candidates were always to be found at all large

gatherings of the people. They were to be seen at barbecues, shooting-matches, corn-huskings, gander-pullings, basket-meetings, public theological discussions, and all sorts of religious and other gatherings of the people. Here they were busy shaking hands with everybody, and using every possible expedient to win their votes. My friend, the late Rev. Dr. W. W. Hill, of Louisville, Kentucky, related to me a very characteristic and amusing incident illustrating this style of electioneering.

While rusticating, quite early in his ministry, at a somewhat celebrated medicinal spring among the hills, he was invited by his host to go with him to a public discussion on the question of baptism, that was to come off in the neighborhood between two distinguished champions, holding opposite views in regard to the "subjects" and "mode" of baptism. Judge C——, a candidate for Congress from that district, who had a very wide reputation as a skillful and successful electioneerer, was present, as polite and busy as possible, shaking hands with everybody, and inquiring with wonderful solicitude after the health of their wives and families. At the close of the services, or, as the people there would say, "when the meeting broke," his host invited the Judge and several of his neighbors to go home with him and eat peaches-and-cream. He said his peaches were very fine, and his wife had saved a plenty of nice cream for the occasion. The invitation was accepted, and a very pleasant party accompanied him to his house. When the company were seated at the table, the Judge found the peaches very rare, the cream delicious, and was profuse in his compliments to both host and hostess. At length the host said :

"Well, Judge, what did you think of the discussion to-day?"

"The discussion," said the Judge, glancing up and down the table, and speaking as if rendering a judicial decision from the bench, "was very able on both sides. The preachers acquitted themselves most honorably, most handsomely. And yet I must say in all honesty that Parson Waller [the Baptist] was rather too much for Parson Clarke [the Methodist]. He had the advantage of him on a good many points. But, then, he had the advantage of him so far as the merits of the question are concerned, *I think.* The Greek settles that question. *Blabtow* may not always, in all circumstances, mean 'immerse,' but *blabtezer,* its derivative, means immerse—go in all over—every time. There's no getting away from that."

"What did you say that Greek word was that always means 'immerse'?" said my friend, the young Presbyterian preacher, a recent graduate of Princeton Theological Seminary, who was sitting immediately opposite the Judge.

"Do you know anything about Greek?" responded the Judge.

"Not much," replied the young preacher.

"Do you know *anything* about it? Have you ever studied it at all?" continued the Judge.

"I have studied and read it some for about a dozen years," rejoined my friend.

The Judge immediately started off upon an episode full of anecdote and amusement, and did not get back to answer the question in regard to the Greek while the company remained at the table.

The Doctor informed me that, as they left the table, he walked off alone into the garden, but was soon overtaken by the Judge, who exclaimed:

"Where did you come from, stranger, and how did you get among these hills, a man that has studied Greek a dozen years? Now let me own up. I don't know a thing about Greek; never studied it at all. I don't know a Greek letter from a turkey-track. I am a candidate for Congress, out on an electioneering excursion. I knew everybody at the table but you, and I saw that it was a Baptist crowd. I wanted to win their favor and get their votes. I heard Parson Smith preach on baptism in the city last winter, and I was giving them his Greek as well as I could remember it. Now," said the Judge, with a jolly laugh at the ridiculousness of his position, "if you let this out on me so that my opponent can get hold of it before I am through this canvass, I'll never forgive you."

It is but simple justice to these Baptists to say

that, had the Judge chanced to dine and eat peaches-
and-cream that day with a company of adherents
of the other champion, his predilections would have
been just as strong in favor of Parson Clarke, and
he would have marshaled his Greek just as positively
in favor of "infants" as "subjects" and "sprinkling"
as the "mode."

I am sure I shall be pardoned if I interrupt the
flow of my narrative to speak of what seems to me
the remarkable fact that, more than forty years after
the scenes I have just described, I am able to say that
the "Parson Smith," so named by the candidate as
furnishing his Greek, was a revered friend whom,
until quite recently, I had not met for more than
twenty years; to whose hospitable home, cheered by
the bright sunshine of one of the noblest and the best
of wives and mothers, I was for years welcomed on
my return from my long horseback journeys, with a
cordiality as warm, I am sure, as though I had been a
member of his own ecclesiastical fold or diocese,
who, now in his eighty-eighth year, resides in New
York City, the honored and beloved senior Bishop of
the Protestant Episcopal Church in the United States.

And I take great pleasure in saying that no
bishop or member of his own Church or any other,
who has not, as I have, often met him in his parochial journeyings, traveled over thousands on thousands of miles of the same indescribably rough roads,

climbed on horseback the same steep mountain-paths,
and partaken of the rough but generous hospitality
of the same rude cabins, can possibly understand
with what patience, with what energy, with what un-
conquerable devotion, he has thus toiled for wellnigh
half a century for the dear Church and the dearer
Master he has so long loved and served with such
pure and glowing love.

One scene in the life of the venerable Bishop is
worthy of the pencil of the most accomplished artist,
worthy to be inscribed upon the walls of the national Capitol as a companion to Bierstadt's "Emigrants crossing the Plains," illustrating as it does
the manner in which the heroic heralds of the cross
have ever accompanied and followed our bold and
daring emigrants, and in every new State laid, broad
and deep, the foundations of learning and religion by
establishing the CHURCH and the SCHOOL.

Having in his extended parochial travels become
painfully conscious of the need of increased efficiency
in the public-school system of the State, he accepted, and discharged for two years—1839 and 1840—
the duties of Superintendent of Public Instruction.
To this work, in addition to his Episcopal duties, he
devoted himself with untiring energy and zeal, visiting and making educational addresses in seventy-six
out of the then ninety-one counties of the State.
Many of these counties could only be visited on horse-

7

back, the only wheeled vehicle ever seen by the inhabitants being the cart in which the laws passed by successive legislatures were transmitted to the different county-seats.

On one of these journeys the Bishop found at a mountain-inn a Methodist circuit-rider, class-leader, steward, and local preacher, assembled for an "official meeting." All hearts beat in the warmest Christian sympathy. As, after a frugal meal, the Bishop's horse was brought to the door, and he was about to renew his journey, all these heroic Christian workers gathered sympathizingly and helpfully around him, one holding his horse by the bridle, another holding the stirrups, and the others helping him to mount. When fairly seated in his saddle, the Bishop reverently uncovered his head, and, lifting his hand to heaven, said: "Send, Lord, by whom thou wilt send, but send help to the mountains!" to which they all responded with a hearty Methodistic "Amen and Amen."

The method of private electioneering by going from house to house, or attending such gatherings unattended by an opponent, was called electioneering on the still hunt. In pursuing the wild game of those regions two methods were adopted. Sometimes the hunters went in large parties, with horses, hounds, and horns, and pursued and killed their game by these public and noisy demonstrations. At other times they went alone and quietly through the fields and woods, came upon their game noiselessly, and killed it by stealth. This latter method was called by the people "*the still hunt.*" In like manner, the politicians had two methods of electioneering, as already described. The one was by public gatherings and by public speeches; the other was by these more private and quiet measures, to which they appropriated this old phrase from the hunter's vocabulary, and called "*the still hunt.*" I remember on one occasion hearing two candidates for the office of sheriff address a crowd in one of the wildest regions in the Southwest, each in advocacy of his own claims. One of them was quite an effective and the other a very indifferent speaker. In a conversation with the former, at the conclusion of the discussion, I told him that, judging from the speeches, and the responses they received from the crowd, I thought his chances must be altogether the best for securing the election.

"Ah," said he, "it won't do to judge by the speeches, or to depend upon them to secure an election. My opponent is the hardest sort of a man to beat. He is powerful on the still hunt."

Many of these candidates displayed most wonderful industry and energy in this "still-hunt" method of electioneering. In a conference with the officers of a county Bible Society, in regard to the time it would take a Bible-distributor to visit every family in the county, for the purpose of supplying them with a copy of the Bible by sale or gift, one of them gave his experience in canvassing the county for the office of prosecuting attorney, told how many families he could visit in a day, and said he thought it would not take the Bible-distributor longer to make his visits than he took to persuade them to vote for him. This was a new and very satisfactory method of arriving at the time really required for a thorough religious canvass of the county.

The "still-hunt" method of electioneering also developed and gave occasion for the display of great tact and skill in influencing every variety of mind and character. Arguments in regard to the questions at issue were often of the least possible influence and importance in securing votes. A lady, whose guest I was, told me that the member of Congress from the district in which she resided, who had been reëlected a great many times, and was at that time Speaker of the House of Representatives, had often visited her house and neighborhood. She said that, when he first began to canvass his district for Congress, he always carried his fiddle with him, and made very indifferent speeches to the people in the daytime, but played the fiddle, greatly to their admiration, for their dances at night. His fiddling and dancing, fine personal appearance, and wonderful skill and tact in mingling with the people and securing their personal admiration and favor, were far more effective than his speeches, and enabled him to "make the race" against all competitors. He was a remarkable illustration of the success of the "still-hunt" method of electioneering. With a most indifferent early education, without a knowledge of English grammar at the commencement of his Congressional career, he was reëlected so often, and continued in Congress so long, that he became perfectly conversant with his duties, served on nearly or quite every committee, was made chairman of the Committee of Ways and Means, became the recognized leader of his party, and was ultimately Speaker of the House of Representatives through two Congresses—from December 1, 1851, to March 4, 1855. With these long years of Congressional experience, he became a very effective stump-speaker, and this, with his "still-hunt" powers, enabled him to secure his reëlection again and again for some thirty years, until he quite wore out the patience of the aspiring members of his own party who were anxious for "rotation" in the office.

After growing gray in the service, he was at length beaten by a youthful member of his own party on this wise: It was one of the established laws of conducting a political canvass of the district that, after the different persons had announced themselves as candidates for an office, no one of them should call a meeting or address an audience in any part of the district without notifying all the other candidates, that they might have the opportunity to be present to answer their opponent and make a plea in their own behalf. A young and aspiring mem-

ber of the party, whose father had grown gray in the
vain hope of a "rotation" in this office in his favor,
determined to take advantage of this "established law"
of the party, and, if possible, secure for himself the office
for which his venerable father had so long waited in
vain. He accordingly announced himself as a candidate
for the office, purchased a very superior horse—there
was then no railroad in the district—published a list of
appointments to address the people of the district at
different places on successive days, but made these appointments so far apart—some eighty miles or more—
that it was impossible for his venerable opponent to ride
the distance. He had complied with the "letter of the
law," but it was one of those cases where "the letter
killeth." Young, vigorous, and possessing great powers
of endurance, he would address the people at one o'clock
in the afternoon, and then make a long ride far into the
night if necessary, and start early in the morning and
ride an equal distance to the next afternoon appointment.
In this manner he canvassed the district alone. He
made his speeches and had no one to answer them. He
had the fullest possible opportunity to tell the people
how long they had honored his opponent, that he had no
further possible claims upon their suffrages, and to make
very earnest and even pathetic appeals in his own behalf.
His venerable opponent was not present to counteract
the force of these appeals, either by the eloquence he
had acquired in Congress, or with his once effective fid-

dle; and so this son of a disappointed office-seeking father not only triumphed in the horseback "race," but "made the political race" for the office sought, and took his seat in Congress. I heard him make several speeches to his constituents, but thought them far less remarkable than the John Gilpin features of his political campaign.

I have already remarked that sometimes as many as half a dozen persons would announce themselves as candidates for the same office at the opening of a political campaign. As the canvass progressed, one after another would become satisfied that his prospects were entirely hopeless, and publicly announce his withdrawal from the race. On one occasion I heard a candidate announce his withdrawal in a speech that I thought described the condition of a great many politicians. It was as follows:

"My fellow-citizens, I came before you at the opening of this campaign and announced myself as a candidate for sheriff of the county. I now appear before you to withdraw from the race. I have a great many friends, strong friends. They stand up to me nobly. Nobody could wish for better friends. There is only this one trouble in my case—*I haven't got quite enough of them.*

"I have already gone so far in this race that I don't know myself. I have lost myself entirely. When I go into the different precincts and hear all the tales that they have got afloat about me, and the character that they give me, it is somebody that I don't know anything about—somebody that I never heard of before.

Fellow-citizens, it isn't me, I assure you, that they are talking about. They have mistaken the man. If any of you should want to know anything about *me*, just ask the boys in my precinct. They know me. They will tell you. They all stand up for me."

I will relate but one more veritable incident to illustrate political life in the Brush, and to show the expedients sometimes resorted to by able and eloquent men to make sure of an election to an important office. I had spent a Sabbath and preached in behalf of the American Bible Society at a small county-seat town upon one of the large rivers in the Southwest. While at breakfast on Monday morning, the circuit judge of that judicial district, who was a resident of the village, sent his colored boy to the house where I was staying, with the message that he had heard that I was going to Big Spring that day, and he wished to know whether I was going in the morning or afternoon. He said that he had expected to go there in the morning, but if he could have my company he would defer his ride. As I had an appointment to meet the officers of the county Bible Society, and attend to the appointment of a Bible-distributor, and order Bibles from New York for the supply of the county, I sent back word to him that I could not close up my business so as to leave until afternoon.

After dinner we mounted our horses and started upon our pleasant ride of about twenty miles. The day was pleasant, the distance not great, the Judge was intelligent and a very fine talker, and I enjoyed the ride greatly. In former visits to the village I had been a guest in his family, when he had been absent from home, holding his courts in distant parts of his district, so that I had not before become as well acquainted with him as I was with his family.

I had been greatly interested and delighted with my long conversations with his venerable mother, and on her account I was very happy to enjoy this long horse-back-ride and pleasant talk with her distinguished son. She was one of the most interesting and remarkable women I have ever met in any part of our country. She was one among the first white children born west of the Alleghanies. Her father had participated in the early Indian wars, and her recollections and rehearsals of the thrilling scenes of early border life and warfare, were the most vivid and interesting of any to which I have ever listened. Born in a frontier cabin, with but few neighbors, surrounded by wild beasts and Indians, the toils, hardships, and excitements of their pioneer life gave little opportunity for education, and she told me that her entire school-life was less than nine months. And yet I have rarely conversed with any one whose language was more smooth, correct, and elevated. The secret of this seemed to lie in the fact that she had read and reread the writings of Sir Walter Scott until not only all his sentiments and characters, but his very style, had become her own. She would repeat his poetry by the hour with wonderful taste and beauty. Scotch blood flowed in her veins, and the warmest love of the fatherland glowed in her heart. With a wonderful command of language, with an easy, elevated, and flowing style, she would for hours together relate the thrilling scenes of her childhood, and the varied incidents of her early border life. Her admiration of her father, and especially of his bravery, was unbounded. I remember the pride with which she told me of a visit she once received from a veteran hunter and Indian fighter, who had been a companion of her father in those early struggles and conflicts, and of the fervor of his parting benediction; "Jenny, God bless you, you are the child of a HERO, as brave as ever shouldered a rifle!"

Kind and genial, as full of sunshine as of stories of the olden time, beloved by old and young, the evening of her life was truly beautiful. Many years have passed since I saw the dear old lady, and I do not know that she is now alive, but I do know that she has not been forgotten. Her measured, flowing periods still roll on in my memory, her quiet, sunny smile beams on me now, as when I sat at her hospitable hearth and board.

I was very happy to have an otherwise lonely afternoon's ride beguiled with the company of the son of such a mother. I had never heard the Judge speak, either in court or upon the stump; but he had an established reputation as an able lawyer and eloquent speaker. I soon found that he had inherited the conversational powers of his mother, and the time wore pleasantly away as we rode on. At length our conversation turned upon the present method of attaining judicial and all other offices, and he gave me the following chapter in his own experience, which I reproduce from memory. In justice to my friend the Judge, I should say that he expressed himself as entirely opposed in principle to an elective judiciary, and gave this chapter in his own experience as an illustration of the way in which even a judicial election *could* be carried.

"I made," said the Judge, "a very thorough canvass of the district with my opponent. We closed our public discussions, and I returned home a few days before the election, which was to come off on the first Monday in August. My opponent was Judge K——, whom you know as a very worthy man, a perfect gentleman, and a superior judge. He was honored by the bar, popular with the people, and a very hard man to defeat. He had held the office several years. I wanted it, had worked very hard for it, and was determined to gain it if possible. I looked over the district very carefully, made the closest estimate I could, and found I should be defeated unless I could make very heavy gains in some precinct. It was a desperate case, and I could in honor only electioneer on the 'still hunt.' I concluded to mount my horse and ride to C—— F——, which you have visited, and know is about the most ignorant and uncivilized region in the State. I thought it more than probable that I would find a barbecue-dance in progress there on Saturday afternoon, at which all the people in the precinct would be present. When I arrived I found a dance in full progress in the open air under the trees, and an ox roasting over the fire near by. It was the last of July, and very hot and very dry. A perfect cone of dust arose above the crowd, in which all the dancers were enveloped. It was a strange, wild scene—a scene to be witnessed nowhere else but in the wildest portions of our southwestern wilds. There were old men and old grizzly-headed women, young men and young women, parents and children, grandparents and grandchildren, all mingling together and dancing with backwoods energy and wild delight. As I dismounted, hitched my horse, and went up and joined those that were looking on, one and another saluted me, very respectfully, with

"'How dy, Broadcloth?'

"As the weather was very warm, I had worn from home a black alpaca sack-coat. This was the only deviation from home-made butternut-colored jeans in the entire crowd. My black coat, therefore, distinguished me from everybody else; and as I walked about among the people the invariable salutation was,

"'How dy, Broadcloth?'

"I moved around among them very quietly an hour

or more, observing all that was going on, and watching
for the most favorable opportunity to make myself known
to them and win their favor. At length my course was
clearly settled in my own mind. I saw what would be
my opportunity. I could see that the fiddler was already
so drunk that he would fall off the block, dead drunk
before a great while. I had learned to play the fiddle
when a boy. I could take the fiddler's place, and prevent the calamity of a complete break-up of the dance.

" His powers of motion failed sooner than I had expected, and there was great sorrow in all the company.
After a while I intimated quietly to some of them that I
could play the fiddle, and they shouted at the top of
their voices:

" ' Broadcloth can fiddle! Broadcloth can fiddle!
Hurra for Broadcloth!' -

" ' At once there was a general rush of the company
about me, all of them imploring me to take the fiddle
and play for them. I replied, very positively:

" ' No, gentlemen, I won't fiddle for you!'

" ' Why not, Broadcloth? Why not?' they all responded.

" ' I will tell you why not,' I said. ' I came here a
stranger, and you haven't treated me with any civility at
all; you haven't invited me to dance; haven't introduced me to the ladies; haven't made me one of yourselves at all; and I won't fiddle for you.'

" But they made so many apologies for the past and

promises for the future that I finally relented, changed my mind, and agreed to fiddle for them. This announcement was greeted with a general shout of joy. I then began to brag in the most extravagant manner possible. I told them that, when they saw me draw the bow, it would be such music as they had never heard since they were born. I took off my coat, unbuttoned my shirt, rolled up my sleeves, took the fiddle, and drew the bow across it, back and forth, for a minute or two, with all my might. They responded to this very noisy musical demonstration with a scream and yell of wild delight and a 'Hurra for Broadcloth!' I took my seat and began to play just before sundown, and played—until the sun was up the next morning. During the night they came around me, and said:

"'Who are you, Broadcloth, anyway?'

"I told them I was a candidate.

"They shouted:

"'Broadcloth is a candidate! Hurra for Broadcloth!' And then asked me what I was a candidate for.

"I told them I was a candidate for circuit judge, and they repeated:

"'Broadcloth is a candidate for circuit judge. Hurra for Broadcloth for circuit judge!'

"This was as much information as I dared to give them in one installment. I did not wish to give them any more until what I had told them was perfectly fixed in their minds, so that they would not make any mistake when they came to vote on the following Monday.

"One of them, a little more thoughtful than the rest, came to me afterward, and, applying an oath to the party to which I belonged, said he hoped I was not a —— ——. I did not, in behalf of myself or party, resent the oath or favor him with any definite reply to his question. I knew that the greater part of the company generally voted with the opposite party, and that, enthusiastic as they now were in my favor, too much information on this point would be fatal to my prospects. I felt quite sure that neither my opponent nor any of his friends would give them this information, and undo the work I had accomplished between that time and Monday morning.

"As the morning dawned, in response to the inquiries of some of the more enthusiastic of my friends, I gave them my name in full, which was greeted and repeated in cheer after cheer.

"When I bade them good-by, mounted my horse and rode away, they followed me with their cheers, and when out of sight among the dense forest trees I could still hear their enthusiastic

"'Hurra for S——, candidate for circuit judge!'

"When the election returns were announced, every vote in the C—— F—— precinct had been cast for me. That night's work with the fiddle secured my election."

CHAPTER X.

SOME STRANGE EXPERIENCES WITH A CANDIDATE IN THE
BRUSH.

HAVING made arrangements with Father E——, a
venerable and faithful Bible-distributor, to canvass a
very rough, wild country, I determined to visit the
county-seat, and address as many of the people as could
be assembled. I did this for the purpose of explaining
to them that the entire State and country were being
canvassed in this manner, for the purpose of supplying
every family that would receive it with a copy of the
Bible, either by sale or gift. As they had been so much
imposed upon by wandering peddlers, I found it very
important to explain to them that it was not a money-
making enterprise—that the books sold were furnished
to them at cost. It was also my invariable custom to
solicit a collection for the Bible Society, wherever I
preached, however poor the people might be. It increased their self-respect to give them this opportunity
to aid in supplying their own destitute poor with the
Word of God.

My ride to B——, the county-seat, was through a rough, wild, and broken region. This may be judged from the fact that the average value of the land, improved and unimproved, of the entire county, as returned by the assessors, and published in the Report of the Auditor of the State for the preceding year, was but one dollar and seventy-nine cents per acre. Even this was a little more valuable than the land of an adjoining county that I explored most thoroughly, the average value of which, as published in the same Report, was one dollar and seventy-four cents per acre. Yet these counties had been settled more than fifty years.

Arriving at the little village, a perfect stranger, my first inquiry was for some professor of religion who would be likely to take an interest in my work, and aid me to make arrangements, if possible, to preach there the following Sabbath. I was directed by my host to call on the school-master of the place, whom I found to be an old man more than sixty years of age, who gave me a warm welcome, and cheerfully rendered me the desired aid. Upon inquiry, we learned that the court-house, which was the place used by all denominations for preaching, would not be occupied the next Sabbath, and accordingly it was arranged that a notice should be circulated that I would preach there on that day, at 4 P. M. This accomplished, I left the village to attend to other duties, and await the Sabbath.

As there was no newspaper at this county-seat, and

but a very few families resided there, and only a few
days intervening, the uninitiated in southwestern backwoods life will wonder how the people in the adjacent
hills and valleys were to be notified of this service and
a congregation assembled. But I had been long enough
in the Brush to have no apprehensions upon this point.
I knew that they would not only all be notified for miles
around, but that the most of them would be present. I
have found by experience that it is one of the peculiarities of the wilder and wildest portions of the country,
that the people will be at the greatest possible pains to
notify their neighbors far and near whenever a stranger
will preach, whatever may be the day of the week or
the hour of the day.

I have frequently arrived at a solitary log-cabin, late
in the afternoon, after a wearisome day's ride through a
rough, wild, mountainous region, and almost as soon as
I had made myself known as a preacher, they would
say:

"Can't you preach for us here to-night?"

"Oh, yes," I have replied; "but I have seen very
few cabins for a long way back, and I can't understand
where the congregation is to come from."

"We know that," they have rejoined; "but there's
a heap of people scattered over these hills, and if you
will agree to preach for us to-night, you will be sure to
have a houseful."

As soon as my assent was given, father, sons, and

daughters have started off in different directions to notify the nearest neighbors, who immediately abandoned
their work to inform other and more distant neighbors.
In this manner all the families over a wide extent of
country would be notified in a short time. Nearly all
would abandon their work, and with it all thought of
supper until they should return, and, taking their children with them, would start at once for the place appointed for the preaching. In such cases I have never
failed to have the promised houseful. Indeed, I have
traveled on horseback over wide regions of country,
where, had I sufficient health and strength, I could have
preached every night to a new congregation assembled
as thus described.

I returned to B——, and reached the court-house
at the appointed hour. The announcement that they
would be addressed by a preacher from L——, the
largest city in the State, had drawn together an unusu-
ally large audience. Before commencing the services, I
was introduced to the county judge, who was also a Baptist preacher. He, with others, had been informed of my
coming, and kindly came to the county-seat, and gave me
the sanction and aid of both his ministerial and judicial
presence. He very naturally assumed the position of
master of ceremonies, and introduced me to his Christian brethren and "fellow-citizens," who not only honored him as their spiritual shepherd, but had elevated
him by their suffrages to his judicial position. He po-

litely escorted me to the judge's seat, which was my pulpit, and sat with me there during the services. This "seat" was simply a high, narrow platform at the end of the room, extending entirely across the court-house, with a railing in front of it, and supplied with benches and a few chairs.

I can not here adopt the very common and convenient expedient of writers, and say that the dress and general appearance of my congregation can be more easily imagined than described. In sober truth, kind reader, granting to your imagination the very highest power, I am constrained to believe that you are entirely unequal to this task. There was very little if any foreign texture there. Their dresses, coats, and other garments had, almost without exception, been spun on their own wheels, woven in their own looms, dyed in butternut from their own hills, and made and fashioned in accordance with their own taste without consulting any fashion-plates. As they were bound by no rules, there was variety, and there were very marked displays of originality. Best of all, there was comfort, and patriotic instincts were gratified by the exhibition of domestic fabrics. It was a rare display of woolsey.

In addressing such an audience the speaker was always gratified and rewarded by the closest attention. I have never seen such listeners as the people in the Brush. They gave a speaker not only their ears but their eyes, and their whole attention. They seemed unwilling to lose a word that he uttered; they yielded themselves to his power. Their faces moved and glowed responsive to his sentiments; and his own mind was animated and enkindled by this sympathy of his audience. I suppose the chief reason of this very marked attention was the fact that the most of these people read very little, and very many of them could not read at all. Hence they acquired the most of their information on all subjects, religious and secular, by being good listeners. Preachers and politicians, the pulpit and the stump, were their chief sources of education. The school and the press were comparatively powerless. Political, theological, and all other controverted questions were settled in the minds of the people by oral discussions. Henry Clay once presided over a theological discussion between the Rev. Alexander Campbell, the founder of the sect popularly known as "Campbellites," and the Rev. Dr. N. L. Rice, of the Presbyterian Church, which was continued through several days, and attended by a large concourse of people. This debate was but a type of hundreds, probably of thousands, that have been held in all parts of the Southwest. Let either a Calvinist or an Arminian challenge the other to discuss the question of the "Perseverance of the Saints," or "Falling from Grace," and, however remote and wild the region, the people for miles around would abandon work and business, and attend for days upon the discussion. Such debates on the question of

Baptism have drawn crowds together in this manner times without number. Any petty lawsuit would bring together the most of the people in the neighborhood, to hear the speeches of the opposing pettifoggers or lawyers. County and circuit-court days were the great days of the year, when the people left their homes *en masse*, and went up to the county-seat in neighborhood cavalcades, and hour after hour, and day after day, listened to the speeches of the opposing counsel. In cases of unusual interest and excitement, such as a murder trial, I have known a very general turnout of the wives and daughters, and have seen them sit for hours together and listen to such speeches. As already described in a previous chapter, political discussions on all questions, State and national, were still more universal and popular, and stump-speeches delivered to these crowds did more to decide the minds of the people in regard to the questions discussed than newspapers and all other causes combined.

This fondness of the people for public discussion, and speeches upon all sorts of subjects, and the remarkable attention they give to a speaker, have done very much to develop the peculiar and often very remarkable oratory that prevailed in these wild regions. Their speakers were so stimulated by the attention given them, and by the visible effects produced by their words, as to draw out all their powers. While they molded the minds and opinions of the people, the people molded their peculiar style of oratory. They acted and reacted upon each other.

It is impossible for a man to become animated and eloquent in addressing an inattentive, listless, stolid audience. I remember hearing in New England a story of the olden time, when, to avoid cooking a Sunday dinner, a pan of pork and beans was put into the hot brick oven, after taking out the bread and pies that were generally baked on Saturday afternoons. The pork and beans were baked in this manner, and taken from the oven for the Sunday dinner. An old divine, remarkable for his eloquence and wit, on one occasion "exchanged" with a brother clergyman whose parish was noted for the production of white beans.

"How did you like preaching for my people?" said the latter, as the two met some time afterward.

"It did very well in the morning," said the witty divine; "but in the afternoon it was exactly like preaching to so many bags of baked beans."

It is not at all strange that in these times there are a good many dull pulpits. There are so many audiences that, either from their minds being absorbed with business or other thoughts, or from sheer mental and physical stupidity, are as irresponsive and as little stimulating to a speaker as "so many bags of baked beans."

But I had no such fault to find with my audience on this occasion. Had there been any inattention, the fault would have been my own. The fact that I hailed from the great city to which they sent their tobacco and other products—the Jerusalem of their affection and State pride—was of itself sufficient to secure me a most respectful and attentive hearing. I had proceeded with the services, and was about half through my sermon, when a gentleman entered the open door of the court-house, halted for a time upon the threshold, and gazed at me for some moments with that excited and intense earnestness with which a stranger is regarded in those regions, where the presence of a stranger is a rare occurrence. He wore a black broadcloth suit, and his appearance and bearing indicated a professional rather than a laboring man of that region. The sheriff's seat was close to the door, at his right hand, and this was occupied by my friend, the venerable schoolmaster of the village, to whom I have before alluded. Turning to the schoolmaster, he plied him with questions for some time, which he evidently answered with great reluctance as he kept his eyes constantly upon me, giving the closest attention to my sermon. At length he turned his head from him, as far as possible, and refused to answer his questions. I had no doubt, from appearances, that in this pursuit of knowledge under difficulties he was seeking information in regard to the preacher he had come upon so unexpectedly. After standing in the door and listening to me for some time, he very deliberately folded his arms, dropped his head in an apparently meditative mood, and promenaded back and forth before me from one side of the court-house to the other. The ladies and a part of the men were within the bar. The rest of the audience were on seats outside the bar, against the walls, and in the windows, so that there was ample room for this promenade over the brick floor in the space between the bar and the seats against the wall. I had had too wide and varied an experience in addressing audiences to be seriously disturbed by this somewhat unusual proceeding, and, as the audience gave me the strictest possible attention, I continued my sermon, and my abstracted friend continued his promenade and his meditations. At length, tossing up his head suddenly, he whirled about, and, moving with a rapid step, marched across the room, passed within the bar, ascended to the Judge's seat, and sat down on a bench at my left hand. After sitting here a while, he lay down and stretched himself at full length upon the bench. Finally he sprang to his feet suddenly, and, evidently supposing that I was concluding my sermon, stepped in front of me, elbowed me back as gracefully as such a thing could well be done in such circumstances, and, bowing profoundly to the audience, he said :

"There is a fine crowd here, and I believe I will make a speech."

This was too much for the patience of my audience, and was greeted by a general and indignant shout of "Sit down! Sit down! Sit down!" from nearly every one present, several of the brethren rising to their feet,

prepared to enforce order by physical force if necessary.
My clerical friend the Judge, who was sitting on my
right, arose with them, and, in the name of law and
order, commanded him to take his seat, reminding him
of the severe legal penalty for disturbing religious worship. Meanwhile I stood a silent and passive spectator
of the scene.

During my sermon I had been struck with the very
marked attention of a rather short, compactly built man,
with very keen, black eyes, who seemed all unconscious
of his very singular attitude. He was in the window, at
my left, nearest the Judge's seat, and had sat through
the sermon, squatted upon his heels, leaning his back
against the window-jam, looking directly into my face,
and listening to every word that I uttered with the most
gratified and animated interest. He was among the first
to spring to his feet, and stood in the window, his black
eyes flashing fire, and evidently more than willing to supplement the Judge's words by any acts that might be
necessary to restore order.

Order was, however, restored without force. My
friend with a speech to make reluctantly resumed his
seat. I resumed and concluded my sermon, and was, in
the vernacular of the people, about to " lift a collection "
for the Bible Society. At this point my oratorical friend
sprang in front of me, and exclaimed, with great vehe-
mence :

" There is a fine crowd here, and I am going to make

A candidate's unsuccessful effort to make a speech.

a speech. I won't be put down by Judge Locke, this man from L——, or anybody else."

This was the signal for the wildest possible excitement. Every man, woman, and child in the audience sprang to their feet, all shouting at the top of their voices,

"Sit down! Sit down! Sit down!"

One immensely tall and large woman at my right, head and shoulders above the group of sisters by whom she was surrounded, with an indescribable bonnet of the largest old-time pattern and a dress of home-made woolsey, in the excess of her excitement and rage, jumped up and down, whirling completely around and jerking her head like a snapping-turtle, and shouted at the top of her voice, which rang sharp and shrill above the general roar,

"Kill him! Kill him! Kill him!"

My friend with the fiery black eyes leaped at a single bound from his perch on the window-sill to the Judge's seat, and seizing the intruder by the collar, jerked him in an instant to the floor below, where he was reënforced by other zealous brethren, among them my host, who was sitting at the opposite end of the room, and together they "snaked" him out of the house in much quicker time than I had ever seen such a feat performed before. The quickness of the whole transaction was wonderful. A part of them took him to the jail, which was but a few yards distant, where he was locked up. Order being again restored, the hats were passed, and I received a collection amounting to about five dollars.

As soon as I pronounced the benediction, the people crowded around me and expressed their intense mortification and sorrow at these occurrences.

" We've got a pretty bad name here anyway," said one, " and if any such thing happens, it is always sure to be when there is a stranger here from a long way off."

" I don't want to fight," said my friend with the fiery black eyes, " any more."

The reverend Judge and the brethren and sisters, one after another, gave expression to their deep humiliation, and my fiery friend kept stepping about nervously, and repeating over and over, half to himself and half to me:

" I don't want to fight any more."

At length, shutting his fist, and bringing it down emphatically, he said :

" I don't want to fight any more. But I won't see religion abused anyway. I will fight for my Master."

Looking at his closely knit, compact form, his quick, vigorous movements, and his flashing eyes, I·could read in his " any more " the story of many a fierce fight before his conversion—which I could not now doubt was genuine.

At length I inquired who the gentleman was that had made the disturbance, and had been so suddenly locked up in jail. I confess I was somewhat surprised to be informed that he was a lawyer and candidate for prosecuting attorney for the county. This was the first

Sunday in August. The election was to come off on the following Monday. He had been making speeches in different parts of the county every day for two or three weeks before. It was very evident that he was not a teetotaler, though, as I afterward learned from himself, he entertained a very high regard for temperance as a theme for oratorical display.

I learned that before sundown his opponent in the canvass magnanimously interposed in his behalf and bailed him out of jail, being chivalrously unwilling to profit by his enforced absence from the polls from such a cause on the ensuing election-day.

After breakfast the next morning, I concluded to walk over to the court-house and see how the election progressed. As soon as I entered the yard, a "sovereign" whom I had not seen before approached me, with a large water-bucket in one hand and a quantity of quarters, dimes, and other change in the other, which he shook before me, and said:

"We are agoing to have a general treat, stranger; would you like to throw in?"

I declined as politely as possible, and he passed on to the tavern to expend the proceeds of his collection for a pail of whisky. "A general treat" is where the whisky is purchased by a "general collection" taken in this way, and put into a water-bucket or larger vessel, and all parties come forward and help themselves with a gourd dipper. A general treat so early in the morning gave promise of a lively day. As I entered the court-house door, my friend the candidate recognized me, and advancing with the most consequential air, and bowing with a great deal of assumed dignity, he said :

"I believe, sir, you are the gentleman from L—— that preached here yesterday?"

I replied, "Yes, sir."

"Well, sir," said he, "I wish to apologize to you. I very much regret what occurred. I came into the court-house, and saw that there was a very fine crowd, and I concluded that I would deliver them a temperance speech. I have a very fine one that I have delivered in Cincinnati, Louisville, and St. Louis, that I was agoing to give them, but they hauled me out like a dog. I am a candidate for commonwealth attorney, sir, and I suppose the affair will injure me somewhat in this precinct; but I think, stranger, that I shall make the race."

Passing through another part of the county some days afterward, I learned that, sure enough, he did "make the race," being elected by a large majority.

It is but simple justice for me to add that, in all my extended travels in the Southwest, this is the only instance where I have had the slightest interruption in the discharge of my professional duties. I have uniformly had that kind, cordial, and hospitable reception for which the people are so justly famed. All my readers will understand that *whisky* was the sole cause of this exceptional case.

CHAPTER XI.

In my extended horseback travels in the Southwest, I made the acquaintance of a great many itinerant preachers, and spent a good deal of time with them in riding around their circuits. I found them, as a rule, a genial, laborious, and self-denying class of men. In general, they had hard work, rough fare, and, so far as this world is concerned, very small pay. But they understood all this when they entered upon this itinerant life. They did not toil for earthly reward. They labored for the salvation of men and the glory of God. Their richest present compensation was the peace and joy that ever pervade the souls of those who, in simplicity and godly sincerity, yield themselves to the toils and privations of this high and glorious calling. In this the richest pleasures and the sweetest joys attend those whose self-denials are the greatest and whose toils are the most severe.

Almost without exception, I found my ministerial brethren in the Brush men with perfect health. This I attributed very largely to their out-of-door life, their horseback-riding, and the fact that they communed far more with men and nature than with books. More than this, I found them cheerful men. They loved and enjoyed their labors. They enjoyed their long rides to preach to a dozen or more at an out-of-the-way appointment—enjoyed preaching, praying, singing, shouting— enjoyed laboring with " mourners in the altar" until late in the night, and they could scarcely speak for hoarseness—enjoyed seeing them "come through" (the vernacular for conversion), hearing them shout, and receiving them into the church—enjoyed class-meetings, quarterly-meetings, camp-meetings, love-feasts, and conference—enjoyed the familiar and affectionate greetings of parents and children, the cordial welcome, and the free and unrestrained social intercourse that awaited them in their pastoral visitations in the Brush—enjoyed with the relish that comes from real health and hunger the "good things" the sisters provided for them, especially *fried chicken.* I have heard it said a great many times that many of the dogs in the Brush knew a preacher as soon as he rode up to a house, and, anticipating the call that was sure to be made upon them, would start out unbidden and run down the chickens for the coming meal, and bring them to the house. I can not vouch for this remarkable canine sagacity of my own knowledge, but I can say that, when riding the circuit with these brethren, I have often seen the

dogs start after the chickens upon a very *slight* intimation, and run them down for our supper as soon as
we rode up, and received from the sister, all aglow with
joy at our coming, the cordial invitation to "'light"
(alight). I speak of all the enjoyments I have thus
enumerated from personal knowledge, for I have
been with many of these good brethren in all these
scenes.

But other and strange scenes were almost constantly
occurring in the prosecution of these labors. On one
occasion I started out with a young preacher to visit
several of his week-day appointments. His circuit was
known in the conference as "Brush College." It was
so called because young preachers, without wife or family, were invariably sent there. They were sent there
if they had a great deal of zeal, and there was any doubt
as to its permanency; for the trials and discouragements
they would there meet would thoroughly test their sincerity and their perseverance. They were sent there if
they were thought to be lacking in humility, or, in the
language of the Brush, if they had the *big-head;* for
roughing it there would be certain to relieve them of
any inflated notions of self. They were sent there not
unfrequently because, in their entire devotion to God and
his service, they were more than willing to go anywhere
and suffer anything if they might lead men to that
Saviour whose love glowed in their souls a pure and
ceaseless flame. Such was the devout character and spirit

of the young circuit-rider whom I accompanied on his week-day visit to Rocky Creek.

It was an intensely hot day in July. As we neared the place of meeting, we passed two or three old women on foot, accompanied by a boy about a dozen years old, who was carrying a brand of fire and swinging it to keep it alive. As the weather was so uncomfortably warm, it was entirely beyond my ability to comprehend what use they could make of fire, and, turning to the preacher, I said,

"What can be their object in carrying that fire with them to the meeting this hot day?"

He smiled as he saw my puzzled look, and simply answered,

"You will soon see."

We rode on to a rough log school- and meeting-house, standing upon the bank of a rocky creek or "branch," as it was called, entirely surrounded by large and small forest trees, under the grateful shade of which we hitched our horses. This was done here, as elsewhere in the whole region, by riding under a tree, pulling down a limb, and making fast to the end of it by a simple loop made with the end of the bridle-reins. This is an admirable method of hitching a horse. The long, easily bending limb offers no resistance to the movements of the horse in fighting flies, and there is no liability of getting the reins or halter under his feet. It has often been a pleasant sight to me to see scores or hundreds of horses hitched in this manner, and standing comfortably in the shade of forest trees, surrounding a church, preaching-stand, or camp-ground. As we returned from this care of our horses, the mystery in regard to the fire was all explained. It had been placed in a large stump, which was burning freely, near the log church. As soon as the people arrived, and had hitched their horses, men and women, old and young, made their way to this stump, lighted their pipes, filled with home-raised and home-cured tobacco, which they carried loose in the ample pockets of their coats and dresses, and sat down on the ground to enjoy a social, neighborly smoke and chat before going into the house to hear the sermon. When the congregation had arrived, by paths radiating through the forest from all points of the compass, some of the official brethren who had accompanied the preachers into the house struck up a familiar hymn. This was the signal for a general laying aside of pipes and gathering in to the service. We had been joined at the church by a "local preacher" who had formerly served in the ranks of the itinerancy, but had "located" in this neighborhood, and, after years of almost gratuitous service in the ministry, was now supporting himself and family by carrying on a small tannery and store. This old itinerant preached the morning sermon. He was a man of strong muscular frame, heavy voice, and great experience and power in moving upon the feelings of his hearers. In the midst of his sermon a woman sitting near me sprang to her feet, threw her arms in the air, and shouted, "Glory! Hallelujah!" and jumped up and down, clapping her hands and shouting until she sank exhausted upon the floor. Soon another and then another, until a large part of the audience were shouting in this manner. The preacher's face fairly glowed with joy, and his voice arose louder and louder as the people were more and more moved; and there was a general blending of songs, prayers, and vociferous shouts. At length, with singing, prayer, and a general shaking of hands, they closed what was to them a very delightful meeting.

In the afternoon, as the day was very hot, it was decided to hold the services out of doors, under the shade of the large oak-trees that stood immediately in front of the cabin. The benches were brought out, and occupied mostly by the women, and the rest of the congregation sat on the ground. I took my position at the foot of a large oak-tree, near the bank of the murmuring stream, and preached to the people grouped and seated before me under the shadow of this and other oaks. All gave the most respectful attention. During my sermon I noticed a woman who was sitting but a few feet distant, and immediately in front of me, hunch with her elbow the one sitting next to her. She immediately hunched in the same manner the next, and she the next, until the, to me, unknown signal had been communicated in this manner to the half-dozen or more who occupied the bench. During this time every eye was fixed on me and not a muscle of any face moved. In a few moments the hunch was repeated, and they all arose from the bench with almost military precision, filed out before me as quietly as possible, moved around to the large burning stump on my right, filled and lighted their pipes, took seats on the ground near by, and all commenced smoking. During all this movement, from the first hunch, they each kept an ear inclined toward me, intent on listening to my sermon, and not one of them apparently lost a word. They smoked on and I preached on to the end of my sermon; and, as usual, "lifted a collection" for the Bible Society, which, in this instance, amounted to about seven dollars. The benediction was then pronounced, and, in their vernacular, the "meeting broke." We spent the night very comfortably with a kind family living near the place of preaching, and returned to continue the services the next day.

In the morning I listened to a sermon from a genuine backwoodsman, the young man I have spoken of in the chapter entitled "The Old, Old Book and its Story in the Wilds of the Southwest," as the guide who piloted the venerable Bible-distributor through that rough, wild region. He had since been licensed, first as an exhorter, and then as a local preacher. It would hardly be possible to find a young preacher whose education had been more completely that of the

Brush. His home was in the wild region I have described in that chapter, and his companions had been as illiterate and uncultivated as could well be found. He had attended school but a very few months, and that was vastly poorer than the most of my readers have ever conceived of as possible. He had then taught, for a few months, this school in his own neighborhood, in which he had received his only education. His reading was tolerable, his writing passable, his spelling horrible. Several weeks afterward I received a letter from him, in which he expressed the hope that certain facts I had asked him to send me would have due weight —which he spelled "dew wate." He was about twenty years old, full six feet in height, with very full, broad chest, square shoulders, and he stood as erect and straight as any Indian. He had a full head of very handsome black hair, bright black eyes, a very mild, pleasant expression of countenance, and a voice that rang loud, smooth, and clear like a trumpet. I listened to his sermon with unbounded amazement, and, I may add, delight. It was a mystery to me how one so unlettered and so unlearned in all religious reading except the Bible—and, in the nature of the case, but poorly versed in that—could have acquired thoughts so sensible and good. It was a greater mystery how he could clothe them in such appropriate language. Both his thoughts and his words flowed as freely as the stream near by, and they had great power to arrest the attention and move the hearts of his hearers.

It was the power of undoubted sincerity and burning zeal; it was the power of one with superior natural endowments stirred to their profoundest depths, and, beyond all question, taught of God. It was the power of one whose life, whose education, and whose modes of thought were in full sympathy with his hearers, who had been born in the same wild region and reared with the same educational surroundings as himself. He was adapted to preach to those people, as the learned pastors of intelligent congregations are adapted to theirs; and each, with his human sympathies, was better adapted to preach to those of like human character and infirmities than any angel in heaven. If it be heresy, I am so heretical as to believe that God has other methods of training some men—yea, many men—to be useful ministers of the Gospel than by filling their heads with Latin, Hebrew, and Greek. So he had trained this man for the remarkable work he had for him to do. Several weeks after this I met him at conference, where he was received into the "traveling connection," to enter upon his four years of practical training and study for the "full work of a Gospel minister." A few months later, in the prosecution of my labors, I reached the circuit to which he had been sent with an older colleague, when I was told by a gentleman of the legal profession that he had often heard him preach, and always with the greatest interest. This gentleman informed me that, while making the round of his extended circuit, his horse had suddenly died. He pushed on on foot to fulfill his appointments, and, on his return, the people had been so gratified with his Christian zeal and energy that they had raised money and purchased a horse, which they presented to him. At the close of the year his report of the numbers converted and received into the church under his labors brought out an emphatic and hearty Amen from the conference. The next year he was sent alone to a rough mountain circuit, where his labors were crowned with still greater success. As long as I was able to trace him, his career was luminous with good accomplished.

But I must return to our services at Rocky Creek. At the conclusion of his sermon several persons were baptized by the old itinerant, who had preached on Baptism the day before. Moving a few steps from the oak where I had preached, they knelt on the edge of the stream, and he stood in the water and baptized them, either by sprinkling or pouring, as they preferred. The entire congregation then knelt with him under the shade of the branching oaks, and he made a prayer so earnest and impassioned that it moved the people to the most intense excitement and joy. The forest rang with their shouting. At the conclusion of this prayer the benediction was pronounced, and the meeting "broke." In all this region meetings were never said to be "out" or to "close." They were said to "break," or, more frequently, "the meeting is done broke." As we mounted our horses I rode with the sister whose hospitality we were to enjoy. She was a woman about thirty years of age, large, and very fine-looking. I had noticed her when shouting, and been particularly struck with the rapt expression of her face. She had a very pretty daughter some fifteen years old. Neither mother nor daughter could read a word. As we rode on she was still much excited with the closing exercises, and speaking of the prayer, she said:

"I thought Brother M—— would pray the limbs off the trees."

When we reached her home, which was an old log-house, she prepared our dinner with the greatest apparent delight. Her house was one of the circuit homes of the young preacher, where he left a part of his clothing. As we were about to leave to attend a quarterly-meeting at the court-house, she called him back, and, in a very frank and motherly way, directed him to make some changes in his dress, saying:

"I don't want my preacher to leave my house looking or'nery."

Afterward I heard of "or'nery" people, "or'nery" preachers, doctors, and lawyers, "or'nery" animals, and "or'nery" almost everything else, and concluded the word was a corruption of "ordinary," though it was more intensely expressive as it was usually applied.

I have been asked by those who were aware of my wide acquaintance with all classes of people in the Southwest, if the character of Nancy Kirtley, in Rev.

Dr. Edward Eggleston's "Roxy," was not overdrawn—if it could possibly be true to nature. I have answered, without hesitation, "It is absolutely true to life." The Methodist sister I have described above was not a Nancy Kirtley in moral character, but she was in personal beauty. In her form and features, in the glow of her face, and in the marvelous beauty of her eyes, she was a remarkable specimen of physical perfection. So was her young daughter, and I have seen scores of others like them in the wilds of the Southwest. I was greatly interested in a distinction drawn by General Grant, when asked if a certain man to whom he had given an office was not a very ignorant man. "He is an illiterate man," said the General, "but I should not call him an ignorant man." That was a "distinction," worthy of General Grant. I have met a great many highly educated literary men who knew almost nothing of men and of the great world outside of books. And I have known a great many illiterate men and women, with marvelous knowledge of the world, with wonderful shrewdness and keenness, and with an ability to compass the end sought surpassed by very few that I have ever known. The fact that they could not read or write required on their part unusual tact and skill not to be overreached, and to make their way in the world. I have known several such men who have acquired large fortunes. Dr. Eggleston's Nancy Kirtley is not a mythical character.

After the young preacher had made satisfactory
changes in his dress, we all bade good-by to our hospitable friends, and rode several miles to the county-
seat where the quarterly-meeting was to commence that
night. Here the young circuit-rider preached the opening sermon, and the meeting continued through the following Saturday and Sunday. There was nothing to me
unusual and noteworthy in the meetings, except in the
love-feast on Sabbath morning. The first to speak was
my host, a warm-hearted, earnest man, a Cumberland
Presbyterian, who spoke of the goodness of God to him
and of his love to all the followers of Christ, and then
started out and shook hands with nearly every one in the
house, continuing his fervent remarks and ejaculations
during all the hand-shaking. Next, a sister spoke and
started in the same manner, shaking hands with the
brethren, and throwing her arms around the sisters and
embracing them in the warmest manner. Nearly all
who followed them went through these same demonstrations. They not only sang,

"Now here's my heart, and here's my hand,
To meet you in that heavenly land,"

but they gave the cordial and often long-continued grasp.
As the experiences, prayers, songs, and shouting became more and more animated and exciting, the hand-
shaking became more general, until nearly the entire
congregation, in larger or smaller groups or numbers,

were shaking each other by the hand, keeping time in their movements to the wild Western melody they were singing. Hand-shaking among brethren and embracing among sisters formed a very prominent part in the religious services of these people in the Brush. This was especially cordial and earnest when one was converted, or, in their language, "came through," after long mourning and praying at the altar. Then parents, brothers, sisters, and warm Christian friends came forward and shook hands with them, or embraced them, amid a general chorus of songs and shouts from rejoicing friends.

As I had now visited nearly every part of the county (including several places to which I have made no allusion), I called a general meeting at the courthouse on Sunday p. m., and organized a county Bible Society. Subsequently, I ordered a large supply of books, and the entire county was most thoroughly canvassed and supplied with Bibles. The results of this work were of surpassing interest, and I shall give some of them in a later chapter.

In my long tours with circuit-riders I was often greatly interested in the accounts they gave me of their experiences upon other circuits. One of them told me that he had joined conference many years before, when he was but nineteen years old. The first year he was sent to one of the roughest mountain-circuits in Tennessee. In addition to the usual outfit, he had a bear-skin

overcoat, so that, if necessary, he might lodge at the foot
of a tree. On receiving his appointment, his predecessor
gave him a map of the circuit, upon which was indicated
all the preaching-places, the families where he would be
most comfortably entertained, and other items to aid him
in the discharge of his duties. I learned that this was
customary at the first conference that I attended, where
I saw the preachers giving the maps they had prepared
of their circuits to their successors as soon as their appointments were read out by the bishop. I was greatly
interested in it, as I had so often felt the want of such a
guide as I had floundered through the Brush, with nothing to indicate where I would find Christian sympathy
and aid in my work. Having reached his circuit and entered upon his labors, he found it necessary to cross a
mountain in order to reach one of his appointments, and
preach to the families that were scattered up and down
the narrow valley and over the mountain-sides. It was a
very long day's ride, and only a mountain bridle-path,
with no friendly family on the route to aid him should
he lose his way. Having reached the top of the mountain, he found several paths leading in different directions, all equally plain, or rather equally blind, and nothing to indicate which one of them he should take. This
was a most uncomfortable dilemma. Himself and horse
were weary with the long ascent, night and darkness
were coming on, and he had no time to lose. He took
one path, followed it to the end, and returned. He took

another and another with the same result. They all led
to where a tree had been cut down for some wild animal,
for bees, or for staves, shingles, or for something else,
either for sale or for the use of the mountaineers. At
length the darkness closed around him, and he made the
best arrangements possible for spending the night upon
the mountain-top. He fastened his horse, made as good
a bed as he could with leaves and the other materials at
hand, and lay down at the foot of a tree, finding abundant need thus early for his bear-skin overcoat. The
night wore slowly away, and he did not like to trust himself to sleep; but, wearied with the toils of the day, it
overcame him, and, as he was falling into a profound
slumber, the terrific yell of a wild-cat broke upon his ear,
and he sprang at once to the back of his horse. Having
no other weapon than a large pocket-knife, he opened
that, determined, as he told me, " to make the best fight
he could with that " in case he was attacked. But he
was spared this. There was no more disposition to sleep,
and he could only watch and wait for the morning. At
length he heard the chickens crowing in the valley below
him, and as soon as it was light enough he started, taking the direction indicated by them. This led him
down the side of the mountain to the family he was
seeking, as directed by his circuit-map. It was near a
large spring, forming the head-waters of one of the important Southern rivers (the Holston). Here he received
the warm welcome that awaits the new preacher on his

first tour around his circuit. Notice of his arrival, and that he would preach at their house that night, was soon sent to their nearest neighbors, and by them communicated to all within reach. They assembled promptly at night, in many instances the parents bringing all their children, old and young. As the different groups arrived, the men invariably brought their rifles and stacked them in a corner of the room as they entered the cabin. At length the room was filled, many of them sitting upon the floor, the children being seated nearest the fireplace. Taking his stand near the chimney-corner, he introduced the services by singing and prayer. As they had no candle or lamp, they prepared for his use a "slut." The light to which they give this not inappropriate name is made by putting oil or tallow in a tea-saucer, teacup, or any bowl or basin they may have, and placing in this a strip of cotton cloth, allowing the end of it to lie over the edge of the dish for a wick, which, when lighted, will burn until the tallow or oil is consumed, affording ample light. Sometimes they take small split sticks, tie them together, and insert the bundle in the tallow for a wick, as a substitute for the cotton cloth. With the aid of this light he was able to "line out" his hymns, and read a chapter in the Bible and his text. In my travels in the Brush I have seen a great many of these "sluts"—to say nothing of others.

At the conclusion of his services no one moved. All sat quietly, as they had during the evening. Now their curiosity must be satisfied. They wished to know all about him, where he had come from, and how he had got there. They were greatly interested in his account of his stay upon the mountain the night before. They knew all about the different paths he had taken, and gave explanations that were quite too late to be of service to him. At length, wearied with his long ride and watchings the night before, he fell asleep upon the bed upon which he had laid down while they were talking to him. In the midst of the night he was awakened by the noise of a terrific rain-storm, and heard the groaning of some animal in great distress near the house. He at once thought of his horse—that he had been hitched without any shelter—and feared that in the storm he had gotten down and was in this distress. An itinerant preacher without a horse in such a region would be in a sorry condition, and he had no time to lose. So, bounding from his bed in the darkness, he made his way to the door, but it was over a mass of human bodies. The entire congregation were asleep, apparently, in the same places they had occupied at the conclusion of his sermon. Instead of his horse, he found that a calf had gotten down, and the water from the roof was pouring upon it. He pulled it out from under the stream, looked after his horse, and returned to his bed. In the morning the congregation slowly dispersed, and he went on his way to other appointments around his circuit.

I was greatly interested and amused with some experiences entirely unlike these, which were related to me by my friend, whom I have already introduced to my readers, the first Methodist circuit-rider that I met deep in the Brush. He had some years before received an appointment to a circuit that was not in the mountains, but in a poor, broken, hilly region of country. Having been provided with a map of his circuit by his predecessor, he was making his way to a part of it known as " Coon Range." Everything indicated the extremest poverty and ignorance among the people. The very small patches of ground cleared and cultivated around their wretched cabins, and the coon, deer, and other skins that were hanging up around them, showed that the chief dependence of the people for a livelihood was upon the chase. Penetrating deeper and deeper into this utterly wild and desolate region, his horse struck and followed a neighborhood footpath until it led him to the back side of a cabin. An opening had been cut through the logs for a small window, but as yet there was no sash or glass in it. The woman, hearing the sound of the footsteps of his horse as he rode up, stuck her head out of this opening, and at the first sight saluted him with,

" How 'dy, stranger, how 'dy? I reckon you are our new preacher."

He told her he had been appointed to that circuit, and gave her his name. At this she was all excitement and joy, and said :

" 'Light, Brother M——, 'light, sir. I'm mighty

glad to see you. Brother K—— used to stay with us a heap, and I've got the 'class-book.'"

As soon as he entered the house she brought the class-book, and began to give him a full account of each member of the class. But he told her it was nearly night, and he had had no dinner. He had ridden all day, and he was very hungry and very tired. She replied to this intimation :

"We'll have supper d'rectly, Brother M——, d'rectly. The pig is in the pen. And Joe, he'll be home right soon, and get the water a bilin'. We'll have supper d'rectly, Brother M——."

To those unacquainted with the people in the Brush, the fact that "the pig was in the pen," and yet to be butchered, would seem to be a somewhat strange reason to give that the supper would be ready "d'rectly." But with her it was a very important advance in that direction. The rest of the pigs, of which I have elsewhere said these people, with little care, raised the greatest abundance for their own use, were perhaps miles away, in some unknown direction, ranging the forest for acorns, beech-nuts, and other "mast" that abounded in that season. "Joe" was such a provident husband that he had gone out and hunted those that belonged to him, called them up to his house, captured and "penned" one of them, perhaps in anticipation of the coming of the preacher. As the supper was so well assured to her, and not dreaming that the delay of a few hours could make any more difference with him than it did with the people in the Brush, she resumed the class-book, and began to go over the names, and tell how this brother could pray, and this sister shout, and how they could all sing, and what happy meetings they had had the last conference year, until he interrupted her with the story of his long ride, great fatigue, and intense hunger. To this she responded, in the most assuring manner:

"We'll have supper d'rectly, Brother M——, d'rect-ly. The pig is in the pen. Joe he'll be home right soon, and get the water a b'ilin', and we'll have supper d'rectly, Brother M——, d'rectly."

Having given him this, to her, perfectly satisfactory and renewed assurance, she went on with the greatest enthusiasm and earnestness to tell him of their love-feasts, and the wonderful "experiences" of some of the sisters, when, in utter despair of getting any supper from this zealous sister, he asked her the distance to the nearest family indicated on his map. She told him it was about three miles. He went out to his horse and mounted it. She followed him with blank amazement, and said:

"Why, Brother M——, you're not agwine, is you?"

He replied:

"Oh, yes, Sister; I must have something to eat," and started off.

Astonished beyond measure, she called after him, and he rode away hearing her emphatic promise:

" We'll have supper d'rectly, Brother M——, d'rectly. The pig is in the pen, and Joe he'll be home right soon, and he'll get the water a b'ilin' d'rectly, and we'll have supper d'rectly, Brother M——, d'rectly! d'rectly! d'rectly!"

Such are some of the experiences I have had with old-time Methodist circuit-riders in the Brush, and such are some of the accounts they have given me of their experiences upon other circuits. They are but specimens of such as were constantly occurring during the months and years of my *ante-bellum* labors in the Southwest. Many of them are so dim and faded on the tablets of my memory that I can not recall them. After so many years, I now, for the first time, record these on more enduring pages, thinking they may afford both pleasure and instruction, and anxious, also, to wreath a garland of merited praise around the brows of those toiling, and too little known, and too little honored circuit-riders in the Brush.

CHAPTER XII.

HEROIC CHRISTIAN WORKERS IN THE SOUTHWEST.

It was a bright, dreamy, autumnal day, that I was making my way among the bayous of one of the most sluggish of the rivers that enter and swell the volume of the Mississippi. My ride since morning had been very long and very lonely. It is a strange sort of life to ride on horseback, week after week and month after month, over a new and sparsely settled country. The most of such journeys are alone. One but rarely meets with company, and then they usually travel together but a short distance before their paths diverge and they separate. In these long, solitary rides, any unusual scene or incident startles one as from a dreamy reverie, and makes a lasting, an almost ineffaceable, impression upon the memory.

I have very often recalled, and shall hardly forget while I live, a most pleasing incident in this day's ride. I had recently traveled over a wide scope of country including a half a dozen counties, where the land was nearly as level as the numerous streams that flowed through it.

The soil was entirely alluvial, and very rich. Occasionally, gentle elevations of a very few feet swelled above the surrounding level, which were crowned with large oaks having short trunks and heavy tops with wide-spreading branches. These oaks were usually interspersed with smaller trees and underbrush. As I floundered through a wet, marshy road, and struck a sandy path leading up one of these elevations, I saw a number of horses hitched to the limbs of the trees, and soon came up to a plain unpainted church or chapel. Its only foundation was the few wooden blocks upon which it stood, and the windows were without sash or glass, the shutters made of boards, being thrown open to admit the light, and closed when the services were ended. I rode under a tree, hitched my horse to a limb, and entered the church as quietly as possible. The preacher had closed his sermon, and was about concluding the services. It was the close of a meeting which had continued several days, in which a number of hardened and very hopeless sinners had been led to Christ. It was his last appointment before leaving them for conference. The labors of the year had left their impress upon his whole frame. He looked wan and worn. He had breathed the malaria of the rivers, bayous, and marshes, along which he had sought out these people in their homes, and near which he had preached to them, until it had changed the color of his flesh to a bloodless saffron hue. I never before or since saw such a human face. It bespoke a body, soul,

A circuit rider in the Brush.

and spirit, heartily, wholly, and irrevocably consecrated to
his noble work. There was over it that perfect calmness
that succeeds long and intense anxiety and excitement,
when their end has been fully attained. As he spoke to
them of the labors of the year, and of his departure for
conference, he was the only one that seemed unmoved.
His voice was low and calm amid the weeping that was
all around him. Among the most noted of the converts
was a woman who for years had done more than any other
person in the neighborhood to counteract the influence of
the preachers who had labored on that circuit, and to injure the little church. She was famous as a fiddler, and
the leader in getting up all the neighborhood dances, and
it was difficult for the young converts to withstand the
fascinations of her bow. In former years she had fid-
dled a great many of them out of the class before their
six months' probation had expired. Now that she had at
last been brought down, there was general rejoicing. It
was like the fall of some tall oak of the forest that
brings down many smaller trees with it. They could
now sing, as I have often heard them in their log-cabins:

> "Shout! shout, we're gaining ground,
>   Oh, glory Halleluyah!
> We'll shout old Satan's kingdom down,
>   Oh, glory Halleluyah!"

This woman sat in a chair near the pulpit (with her
little babe lying, smiling and playful, upon her lap), par-
ticipating with the deepest interest in all the services,

and weeping among those most deeply moved. At the conclusion of his remarks the preacher baptized this little child, the mother giving to it the double name of himself and his colleague on the circuit. His work thus ended, he sang alone, in a clear, firm voice, a simple and beautiful parting hymn, that I can not now repeat, with the refrain,

"Brothers, fare ye well,"

passing at the same time through the congregation and shaking hands with the weeping class-leaders, stewards, local preachers, and other brethren present. He then moved to the other side of the room, and sang on in the same manner, changing the refrain to,

"Sisters, fare ye well,"

and shook hands with each one of them, he alone being perfectly calm amid their convulsive weeping and sobs. The benediction was then pronounced, and I withdrew as quietly as I had entered, and resumed my journey. Such labors in such a region illustrate a moral heroism that is both heroic and sublime.

REV. JAMES HAWTHORN, D. D.

I recall a very different experience with another type and class of these heroic workers for the Master.* Many

* The late Rev. James Hawthorn, D. D., of Princeton, Kentucky. Every word of this record of his heroic labors was written while he was yet alive, and I did not wish to startle or offend his sensitiveness and modesty by giving his name to the public. But, now that he has gone to his full

years before, he mounted his horse and rode from his home in the Southwest, over the Alleghany Mountains, onward to Philadelphia, and thence to Princeton, New Jersey, where he sold his horse and spent three years in the Theological Seminary. He had then returned, and spent his ministerial life in preaching to feeble congregations that were able to pay but a small salary for his services. At the time I first met him he preached regularly on alternate Sabbaths to two congregations about twenty miles apart. In those months in which there was a "fifth Sabbath," he usually visited some yet smaller congregation, often at a greater distance, for the purpose of preaching to them, and perhaps administering the communion and baptizing their children. But this was only a small part of the labor he performed. The compensation he received for these services was entirely inadequate for the support of his family, and he was obliged to supplement his salary by other and more arduous labors. He spent five days each week in teaching a school in the basement of his church. And they were not such days' work as are usually given to teaching. Immemorial custom in that region had required of teachers nearly as many hours' daily labor in the school-room as were

and glorious reward on high, I am most happy to pay this tribute of abounding veneration and love to this noble servant of our common Master. As his compensation for his purely missionary services was so very small, I once took the liberty of suggesting that he should receive a stipend from the Presbyterian Board of Home Missions. It was most respectfully, but positively declined. That was the true Pauline spirit of the man.

given to any other employment. Hence he usually began his labors in the school at or before eight in the morning, and did not close until five, or later, in the afternoon. His scholars were of all ages and grades of attainment, and they pursued a great variety of studies. Many of both sexes studied the higher English, classical, and mathematical branches, and completed their education at this school. This diversity in the ages of the scholars and the books they attempted to master added greatly to his labors; but from early Monday morning until late Friday afternoon he toiled faithfully in the school-room, term after term and year after year. With all this teaching, he had the other labors indispensably connected with such a school—the care of the school-room, consultations with parents, the collection of bills, and all the nameless calls and duties connected with its care and government. When to the long rides and other labors as a pastor, and the duties of a teacher, that I have enumerated, are added those of a housekeeper in providing for his family, there would seem to be little time left for the preparation of sermons. But these were thoroughly studied, and very often fully written, in hours that most others would have given to rest and sleep.

On a cold midwinter day I mounted my horse and rode with him some twenty miles to his regular appointment on Saturday afternoon. When we reached the log-school-house in the outskirts, of his congregation but a small number had come out through the cold, and at his request I preached to them. We then rode home with an old Presbyterian elder, the cold constantly increasing in severity. His heart was much warmer than his log-house. We slept in a room which he tried in vain to warm with a large wood-fire. But the water we were to use in the morning froze solid, though placed as near the fire as possible. After breakfast we mounted our horses and rode a few miles to church, though it was so cold that I nearly froze in going, and was obliged to stop on the way to warm myself. I preached to a congregation of about forty, and we reorganized the county Bible Society. Having kindly rendered me all the aid in his power, he mounted his horse after dinner, and rode home through the cold in order to be able to open his school promptly on Monday morning. At other seasons of the year, when the weather was such that the people could assemble for worship, he was accustomed to preach at the church in the morning, and at some school-house like that in which I had preached, in other and distant parts of the congregation, late in the afternoon. He would then mount his horse and ride over the roughest roads, often through mud, rain, and darkness, reaching home late at night, so that without fail he might promptly open his school the next morning. I inquired and learned of others the salary that was *promised* him for preaching in this manner to this congregation, twenty miles from his home, twice each month. I would state the amount, but I remember the story, told me by my genial friend, the late Rev. Dr. William L. Breckenridge, of an Irishman who desired to have a letter written home to Ireland from Kentucky, many years before, when provisions were most abundant and cheap.

After mentioning a good many things that he wished him to write to his friends in regard to America, he said:

"Tell them that I get all the meat I can eat three times a week." ·

"And what do you mean by that?" said his employer. "Don't you get all the bacon you can eat three times a day?"

"Yes, your riverence," was the prompt reply.

"Well, then, what do you mean by writing to your friends in Ireland that you get all the meat you can eat three times a week?"

"Faith," said Pat, "and *that* is more than they will belave."

But these were not the hardest and most poorly remunerated of the labors of my friend. In some of his visits to smaller congregations on the "fifth Sabbath" his rides were much longer, and he encountered difficulties and discouragements such as most Presbyterian ministers have never dreamed of. I will relate a single case. A small church some fifty miles distant was without a pastor, and for a long time the sacrament of the Lord's Supper had not been administered

to them. Always ready to aid and cheer such strug-
gling churches, he promised to give them a "fifth Sabbath." I will here say that there were hundreds of
churches of different denominations in the Southwest
and South that did not have preaching every Sabbath.
They enjoyed this privilege but twice a month, once a
month, or less frequently. When their appointments
for preaching were regular, the *number* of the Sabbath
in the month was always specified, as, for instance, the
first and third Sabbaths might be the days selected for
preaching regularly at one church, and the second and
fourth Sabbaths might be appropriated to two other
churches. Or the first, second, third, and fourth Sabbaths might be the days fixed for regular preaching,
once a month, at four different places. And so of
all week-day appointments for preaching. They were
always made for some day in the first, second, third, or
fourth week in the month. Hence the people did not
need to consult an almanac in regard to the day of
the month, and there was rarely any mistake or confusion in regard to these appointments. Where several different denominations occupied the same court-
house or building for preaching on successive Sabbaths,
this was a matter of great importance. It always stirred
bad blood when from design on either part these appointments conflicted, or, in the language of the Brush,
"locked horns." From the simplicity of this method
of making appointments the people would learn for

miles around, and remember for months ahead, that a basket-meeting, sacramental meeting, or camp-meeting would commence on the second Friday in August, or the third Thursday in September, or any other day that was announced in this manner. As the "fifth Sabbath" is of infrequent occurrence, young preachers often took this day to visit their mothers and sweethearts, and old preachers made missionary tours and visited neglected neighborhoods and destitute churches. It was such a day and such a work my worthy friend had promised the little church to which I have alluded. After his accustomed labors for the week, he on Saturday performed the long, rough horseback ride, and on Sabbath preached and administered the communion to them. But it was not a pleasant service. The day was cold; the church, like others I have described, had no other foundation than blocks of wood; the hogs of the neighborhood had made their bed under it, and they successfully disputed all efforts to drive them from their warm shelter. Hence all the services of preaching and the administration of the Lord's Supper were performed with the accompaniment of their incessant squealing and fighting immediately under the pulpit and communion-table. The long, cold ride home extended into the darkness of midnight. How few have ever gratuitously performed so laborious a service with so little to compensate, so much to sadden and distress!

But such experiences were relieved by many of a far

different character. To many feeble churches his coming was anticipated by all needed preparations, and he was greeted with great joy by the little flock. They listened with delight to the truths that they loved as they fell from his lips. Cheerful homes welcomed him and were gladdened by his presence. To many scattered families of the church to which he belonged his pastoral visits were all that they received, and they were the more prized because such visits were so rare to them.

Faithful, laborious, self-denying man of God! his toils have not been unrewarded in the past, and they will be abundantly honored in the future.

CHAPTER XIII.

STRANGE PEOPLE I HAVE MET IN THE SOUTHWEST.

I HAVE met a great many very odd and strange characters in the Southwest. The peculiar life of the people developed their originality. They were not restrained by the laws and customs that control older and more established communities. Every man was a law unto himself. All that was unusual and peculiar in their natural characters grew in unrestrained luxuriance like the wild vines on their hillsides and in their valleys. What any man or community might think of their actions or mode of life had the least possible influence in deciding what they should do or not do. The laws of fashion, generally so tyrannical, were utterly powerless with them. What any one else might think of the color, shape, or quality of a garment, had no effect upon them. They dressed entirely in accordance with their own notions of comfort. This same kind of independence characterized all their actions and their entire life.

I frequently passed the plantation of a very marked character of this peculiar type, who, by great energy and native shrewdness, acquired a large property, and became the owner of many slaves. His dress and personal appearance were such that strangers calling at his house on business often mistook him for a plantation "field-hand," and called on him to open the gate leading to his residence, or for any service they would expect from a slave. He could read and write, but his spelling was about as bad as possible. On one occasion he wrote an advertisement and took it to a printing-office. The proprietor, knowing his positive traits of character, told him as politely as possible that there were some mistakes in the spelling, which, with his permission, he would correct in printing the advertisement. The old man was as positive and unyielding in regard to his spelling as in regard to his dress and everything else, and would submit to no changes. That was his way of spelling, and his way was as good as anybody's way. It must be printed exactly as he had written it, or not at all. It was so printed; and in addition to the amusement it afforded to the people of that region, a copy was sent to a large museum in a Southwestern city, and was among the most amusing of all their curiosities.

In a long horseback-ride over a turnpike-road connecting two large Southwestern cities, I stopped to dine and feed my horse at a house of entertainment. Entering a small apartment that served for a sleeping-room for the family and a sitting-room for travelers, I met a sight very unusual in that region. I found the walls of the room covered with a large number of cheap lithographic portraits of the prominent statesmen and military heroes of the country. A very brief interview showed me that my host was "to the manner born," and a very striking and original character. At length I alluded to the portraits hanging about his room and said:

"You seem to be very fond of pictures, sir."

"I am a patriot, sir," he replied.

Feeling quite sure that I should get a positive opinion, without any sort of hesitation I said to him:

"And who, sir, do you think was the greatest man of all the Presidents, statesmen, and military and naval heroes whose portraits you have here?"

"Andrew Jackson, sir," was the prompt reply.

"Ah!" said I, "I see, sir, that you have the portrait of Washington. Was Andrew Jackson a greater man than George Washington, sir?"

"I tell you, sir," said he, "Andrew Jackson was the greatest man God ever made. He was a man of firmness—more firmness than Washington."

Greatly to my surprise, I had found lying open upon a bed in our sitting-room a copy of Mrs. Harriet Beecher Stowe's "Key to Uncle Tom's Cabin," but recently published, the only copy I ever saw in that region. I made some inquiries in regard to it, and he told me he had bought it of a Jew peddler who had spent a night with him. He was very much absorbed in reading it.

"I tell you, sir," said he, "the man that wrote that book was a very smart man. They say 'twas a woman; but I tell you, sir, the man that wrote that book was a very smart man." In all our long conversation he did not give the slightest possible credence to the idea that the book had been written by a woman. His oft-repeated and invariable statement was:

"I tell you, sir, the man that wrote that book was a very smart man. They say 'twas a woman; but I tell you, sir, the man that wrote that book was a very smart man."

A large number of his slaves were passing in and out of the room, preparing our dinner. At length he said to me:

"I tell you, stranger, that is my greatest trouble. What is to become of these people when I am gone?"

I knew that the laws of the State forbade his emancipating and leaving them there, and so I said:

"I suppose you know that some masters are freeing their slaves and sending them to Liberia."

"I know that, sir," said he, "and I have told mine that I would free them all and send them there if they would go. But they have told me they would rather I would chop them into mince-meat than go there."

Their ears had been filled with such tales in regard to Liberia that this was their idea of the place. As I never saw the old man but this once, I do not know what became of him or his slaves.

In former chapters I have spoken of my visit to a celebrated watering-place. I met there some very strange characters. My sermon in a "ballroom" was preached at this watering-place. I found it much more of a resort for gamblers than clergymen. In the general suspension of travel on the Southern and Western rivers, on account of the low stage of the water, and other causes, the gamblers, who usually plied their vocation upon the river-steamers, congregated in large numbers at these Springs. The waters were famed for cleansing the system, and preventing malarious diseases. In addition to this improvement of their health, and preparation for the renewal of their usual employment on the steamers, and at the cities and towns along the rivers, they found many subjects upon whom to practice their arts successfully, among the numerous and often verdant visitors at the Springs.

Wishing to avail myself of the benefit of these waters, I spent some two or three weeks here, visiting meanwhile a large number of neighborhoods in the vicinity, in the prosecution of my labors. I witnessed here the most remarkable devotion to card-playing that

I have ever seen or known. The principal sleeping-apartments for the hundred or more guests were in a long, low, log structure, but a single story high — a series of cabins—with a piazza along the whole front which served as the general promenade for the visitors. In going to and from my room, day after day, I passed a table standing upon this piazza, within a foot or two of my door, which was surrounded by card - players. The principal character at this table was an old, gray-headed man, apparently not less than seventy years of age. In the morning he always accompanied his wife to the dining-room, and, as they returned from breakfast, they separated at the door, and she went alone up the piazza to her room, and he walked down the piazza in the opposite direction, and took his seat at this card-table. It was the hottest July weather, and the old man took off his coat and vest, rolled up his shirt-sleeves above his elbows, and sat down and played cards, without any interval, until the first bell rang for dinner. He then went to his room and waited upon his wife to the table. As they returned, he parted with her at the door of the dining-room, as after breakfast, walked down to his card-table, disrobed himself, and took his seat as in the morning, and played without cessation until the first bell rang for supper. He then went to his room and waited upon his wife to the table as before. This was repeated, with unfailing regularity, day after

day, and week after week. I was told that he was
not a professional gambler. As I passed the table,
which I was compelled to do every time I went to
my room, there was not usually a great deal of
money lying upon it at stake in the game—only
" enough to keep up the interest and excitement."
But sometimes there were piles of gold lying over
the table, and they seemed to be gambling in earnest and for large amounts.

The devotion of this old man to cards or gambling
was so remarkable that I confess I was somewhat surprised to see him enter the ballroom with his wife
among the first of those who assembled to hear me
preach on the Sabbath. I had preached at a court-
house, a few miles away, in the morning, and returned
here to address the people at four in the afternoon.
There was a general attendance of the visitors, including the well-known professional gamblers, and all gave
me as respectful a hearing as I could desire. I was
furnished with a Bible for the occasion, but there was
no hymn-book. I expected to resort to the expedient
of "lining out" some familiar hymns, which was the
most frequent method of singing in this region. But
the old card-player came forward to the table where
I was sitting, and handed me an Old School Presbyterian hymn-book, which I had seen his wife bring into
the ballroom, and which she sent up for my use, as
she saw there was no hymn-book on the table. Some

months after I recognized the aged couple in a large
city congregation to which I was preaching, and was
afterward told by its honored and beloved pastor that
the old man was one of the most regular and attentive attendants at his church, and that his habits as I
have described them were widely known. His manner was so apparently reverential, and his attention so
marked, that strangers preaching there often got the
impression that he was one of the elders of the church.
So strange and paradoxical are the " characters that
make up the world."

Among the visitors at the Springs was one who was
a very wealthy man, a large slaveholder, and a very
great invalid. He was a cripple, with one limb much
shorter and smaller than the other, and was compelled
to use two crutches to walk at all. As I saw him
mingling with the visitors, I observed that he was
profane, rollicking, genial, and exceedingly social in
his nature. I do not now remember how I became
acquainted with him, or whether or not I was introduced to him at all. But from the first he attached
himself to me, and sought my company. If I sat
down alone upon the piazza, he would come and take
a seat near me, and we engaged in long conversations.
I explained to him in the greatest detail the work in
which I was engaged, and the operations of the American Bible Society at home and abroad. I described
to him the Bible House in New York, and the proc-

ess of making Bibles—commencing with the printing of them in the higher stories, and passing them through different hands from story to story below, until they reached the depository, well-bound and beautiful specimens of the art of book-making. I told him of the wealth and business character of the men who acted as managers of the society, and gratuitously supervised and controlled all its operations. Thoroughly irreligious in all his training and associations, my statements were new to him, and he was greatly interested in them. He thought the whole thing was "grand" and "magnificent," and was enthusiastic in his commendations of me and my work. When I was absent for a day or two for the purpose of meeting the people of some neighborhood at a week-day appointment, he was among the first to meet me on my return to the hotel, and inquired with the greatest interest as to the success of my labors. In our repeated interviews I talked with him frankly, freely, and fully, in regard to his own spiritual condition, urged him to make religion a personal matter, yield his heart to Christ, and live henceforth for the glory of God, and the good of his fellow-men. The openness of his nature and the frankness of his expressions upon this subject were remarkable. His belief in the Bible was implicit. He did not seem to have a shadow of doubt in regard to its truth. He told me that, from the nature of his disease, he was liable to die at any moment, and if he died he knew he should be lost. He did not seem to have a particle of doubt on this subject. Sometimes, in deep consciousness of the struggle within him, he would say:

"The trouble with me, sir, is, that I have no stability—I just go with the crowd I am in. When I am with a man like you, I wish I was a Christian. I would give the world to be a Christian. But when I am with W—— and G——" (naming the chief gamblers at the hotel) "and their crowd, I am just carried away with them. I can't help myself. If I could always be in the company of men like you, I believe I could be a good man and a Christian."

I prayed with him in my room at different times, and gave him all the instruction and encouragement in my power.

On learning from me that I was a native of the State of New York, and was familiar with the free States, he had a great many questions to ask in regard to them. He had never been out of the slave States. He inquired particularly in regard to the schools, and whether there were any schools where colored boys could be educated. I gave him the name of Oberlin and other schools that then admitted colored students. He told me that he had been confined to his bed seven years; that the greater part of the thigh-bone of one of his limbs had come out; that his body-servant had nursed, washed, and taken care of him like

10

a baby all this time; and that in reward for these services he had offered to grant him and his two boys
their freedom, and give the boys a good education.
" But," said he, " I don't hire any overseer now. He
is my overseer, and that makes him the biggest nigger
in T—— County, and he says he ' don't want no freedom,' but he would like to have his boys sent to school.
Now, sir, if you will find any school in the North that
will take them, I will send them to school just as long
as there is any use of their going."

I afterward wrote to several institutions on the subject, and sent their replies to him at his home. He
was very anxious to know positively if he could send
them to the State of New York, and said : " I can not
send them to Illinois or Indiana, and I can not understand how they can be sent to New York. They are
all free States." I told him that Illinois and Indiana
had passed laws prohibiting colored persons coming into
those States, but New York had not. He then wanted
to know why this was so, and I told him that one
reason was, that New York was so much farther from
the slave States, and less likely to be overrun by free
colored people. He at length became satisfied upon
this point, a very important matter with him, as the
sequel will show.

On one occasion, in explaining to him the nature
of my Bible-work, and the extent of the territory committed to my supervision, he interrupted me with—

" That will include T—— County, my county. You must certainly come and see me when you reach that part of the State, and stay with me while you are in that region."

I thanked him for his invitation, and told him that I should be certain to call on him. This invitation was often repeated, and renewed with special earnestness when we separated. A long time elapsed before I visited all the intervening counties, organized or reorganized Bible societies, preached and " lifted collections " in the more important churches, ordered Bibles from New York, secured the appointment of colporteurs, and completed all the arrangements for a thorough canvass and supply of the counties. But after several months I reached T—— County ; and, as my friend resided some distance from the county-seat, I completed all my arrangements for the supply of the county before making him my promised visit. This accomplished, I mounted my fleet horse and rode several miles to his residence. His welcome was as warm, cordial, and hearty as words and acts could make it. A long-absent brother could not have been received with greater demonstrations of joy. After I had laid aside my leggins and spurs, washed myself, and a troop of big and little house-servants, who were rushing about eager to render some service in welcoming me to their master's hospitalities, had brushed me and properly cared for all my wants, and the commotion created by the arrival of a stranger at a large plantation had somewhat subsided, my host said to me :

"The blue - grass in my pastures is knee-high to your horse. Now just stay with me a few weeks, and let your horse run there. The weather is hot; you are a hard worker. You need rest, and your horse too. It will do you both good. Just stay with me, and I will kill my biggest, fattest turkeys, and give you the very best that the plantation affords."

I thanked him for his cordial welcome, told him that I could not spare so much time, but would stay with him as long as I possibly could.

He then inquired after my plans for the supply of his county with Bibles. I told him that I had spent the previous Sabbath at the county-seat, and gave him the names of all the men that had been elected as officers of the County Bible Society, and of the colporteurs that had been chosen to canvass and supply the county. He knew them all, and approved the choice that had been made. I then said :

"I have ordered a large supply of Bibles from New York, and I am quite sure I can depend upon the people of the county to meet the expenses of this work."

"Yes," said he, thrusting his hand into his pocket, and taking out and opening his pocket-book, and handing me a bill, "there is twenty dollars for T—— County"; and, handing me another bill, "There is ten dollars for the world."

I was very much gratified with his appropriation of the money, as I saw that, in my conversations with him, I had given him a clear idea of the local or home work and the general or foreign work carried on by the American Bible Society.

A bountiful supper followed, and the evening passed very pleasantly and rapidly in conversation; with many reminiscences of our life at the Springs, and the various persons we had met there. At length he ordered the Bible brought forward, and the servants summoned for prayers. A large number, including the house-servants, and their husbands and children who lived in the kitchen and other adjacent buildings, were soon assembled. The master and myself were the only white persons in the group. He sat near me in a large chair, thin, pale, and sickly, his two crutches lying across his legs, and seemed profoundly interested and impressed. With a stillness that was almost motion-less and breathless, and with a fixed, an earnest, an excited attention, such as I have never seen, only as I have seen it in many similar groups, they all listened while I read to them a portion of the blessed Word of God—that Word that I have found so potent to soothe and cheer and bless the most ignorant and the most oppressed — and then we all bowed together before our common Father, and in language as simple as I could command I earnestly besought his blessing to rest upon them all, and commended master and slaves to his compassionate care and love. As, after the lapse of so many years, the long-closed chambers of memory open at my bidding, and, recalling this scene, I for the first time commit it to pages that can be read by others, it all stands revealed before me, so vivid, so *present*, so unspeakably tender and precious in its memories, that again and again I have been compelled to lay down my pen and wipe the fast-falling tears that would flow as I have lived over again the golden, glorious hour thus spent in communing with God and comforting his enslaved and suffering poor. The same divine power comes down upon me now, while I write, as when I knelt in the midst of that dark group, melting my soul with a tenderness so inexpressibly sweet, and irradiating my whole being with a joy so unearthly that I can but exclaim with the poetess:

> "Tell us if the gleams of glory,
> Bursting on us when we pray,
> Are not transient, blest revealings
> Of our *home*, so far away;
> Loving glances of our Father,
> Sent to lure our souls away."

A delightful night's rest was followed by a most beautiful day. A morning stroll revealed to me the character and extent of my host's plantation. His residence was a large brick house, standing in the midst of a grove of forest-trees, and presented a most neglected, not to say dilapidated, appearance. A great many panes of glass had been broken from the windows; the doors were out of order; it had been unpainted for many years; the fences, out-buildings, and everything about it had a "tumble-down" look, and all presented about as "shiftless" an appearance as ever distressed the soul of a neat and thrifty Miss Ophelia. If my memory is not at fault, the plantation contained one thousand acres. It was as rich, productive, and beautiful land as I have ever seen. It lay in the heart of one of the finest tobacco-growing regions in the United States. The stock, most of which was "blooded," and of the finest quality, presented noble subjects for the pencil of a Rosa Bonheur, as they were feeding in his large pastures, where the blue-grass was up to my horse's knees. The buildings I have already described sadly marred a landscape of exceeding beauty. This was the paternal estate. He had lived with his parents until their death, and, being the youngest son and an invalid, they had given him the homestead, providing liberally for the other members of the family, who lived in adjoining counties and were very wealthy. The place was cultivated by his own slaves, who, including old and young, I think must have numbered nearly or quite a hundred.

Shall I describe the household?

My host was unmarried. I do not know his age.

I remember that his hair was so much frosted that it was decidedly iron-gray; but I am sure that it must have been prematurely so, on account of the great suffering he had endured. His housekeeper was a large, fat, gross-looking negro woman, one of his own slaves. But she was more than his housekeeper—she was the mother of his children. Here was one of those strange, unaccountable, revolting alliances—far more common than the great world has ever dreamed—that set at defiance the laws of God not only, but all other laws —where the one least attractive of all upon the plantation becomes the master's unholy choice. It hardly required the second look to detect among the groups of colored children that were playing about the yard four who bore to their father the double relation of children and slaves. The two eldest were girls, probably six and eight years old, and they had his light gray eyes, his double chin, and, indeed, all his features much more strongly marked than is usual where both the parents are either white or black. In their color, his white blood preponderated very largely over that of the mother; their hair indicated their African parentage much more positively than their skin. The two boys were much darker than their sisters, and the features of their father were less strongly though indisputably marked. The youngest was a handsome little fellow not more than three or four years old.

Here, then, to any one who had seen but a tithe

of what had fallen under my observation in years of horseback-riding where I had been in constant communication with masters and slaves, was the full explanation of the intense interest and anxiety of my host in regard to the *schools* and *laws* in the free States. Here was a mind agitated with the most terrible conflicts, the most excruciating anxieties, that ever raged in the human heart. Here were the pangs of a guilty conscience in regard to the past; and all the instincts of a father moved to their profoundest depths in behalf of his children, who were legal slaves. He knew, even better than I did, the unutterably terrible future that awaited them as slaves. He knew not only the possibilities but the probabilities in regard to the fate of his daughters, which the laws and the customs of society rendered doubly sure. It was to a mind thus agitated and distressed that I had brought the sweet message, "The blood of Jesus Christ cleanseth from *all* sin." It was to a spirit thus moved that I unfolded the fullness and the freeness of the forgiveness and salvation purchased by the sufferings and death of the "Lamb of God that taketh away the sins of the world." It was to one thus involved and entangled in the meshes of sin that I spoke of a Deliverer from its thralldom and power. O wondrous message! Often as I have looked into the faces of the vilest of the vile, I have been thrilled and startled at the sound of my own voice as I have proclaimed to them: "Though your sins be as scarlet, they shall be as white as snow; though they be red like crimson, they shall be as wool."

No wonder that he listened intently, and that his eyes often filled with tears, as I sat long at his bedside, where he was compelled to lie the greater part of the time, endeavoring to instruct him and lead him to Christ. If I were to repeat all the strange questions that he asked and that I answered—questions the like of which I never heard of being propounded to a minister of the gospel before—they would be far more strange and startling to my readers than anything I have written. No wonder that he esteemed and loved me as he did! Probably no clergyman had ever treated him with that consideration or instructed him with that care and earnestness that I had.

Possibly if I had known as much of his character as I afterward learned, I should have been less enthusiastic and hopeful in my efforts to instruct him and lead him to Christ. But it has been one of the incidents of my long wanderings and extended intercourse with strangers, that I have made the acquaintance of negro-traders, slave-hunters, gamblers, and other like characters, enjoyed their hospitality, prayed with and for them and their families, and given kind and hopeful words of instruction, where those who knew these people best had little heart or hope to put forth such efforts in their behalf. At times I have been permitted and rejoiced to learn that such labors have been attended with the happiest results.

When I asked the officers of the Bible Society the way to the residence of my friend, and told them of my promise to make him a visit, the strange, blank expression upon their faces told me plainly that his home was not a resort for clergymen. Their silence on the subject was far more expressive than the few ejaculations of surprise that were uttered. No wonder that he took such strange ways of manifesting his affection and regard. Once he called a servant and gave directions to have two white shoats thoroughly washed in soapsuds, and driven up to the front door for me to look at. He told me he had sent to Marshall P. Wilder, near Boston, Massachusetts, for a pair of white pigs and a pair of chickens, which with the freight had cost him a large sum, which he named, but which I have forgotten. He was anxious to gratify me by seeing them in the best possible condition. Indeed, he seemed never to forget that I was his guest, and he was constantly striving to do all in his power for my entertainment, and to render my stay with him as pleasant and protracted as possible. Very often he would repeat what he said to me so frequently at the Springs :

"If I could only have none but good people for associates, I believe I could be a good man. But I haven't got a bit of stability. I am just carried away by the crowd I am with. If I could only have you here, I believe I could be a Christian. If you will only stay here and preach for us, I will give the ground for a church and help build it, and I will bind my estate for a part of your salary after I am dead and gone, as long as you will stay. The trouble is now, if we do go to church, any one else there might just as well get up and preach as the man that does preach.* You are an educated man, and I believe you are a good man; and then you are a gentleman. If they would only send such preachers into this country, I tell you they would take the crowd. My mother was a Baptist, and I believe she was a good woman, and if I was fit to belong to any church, I should like to join the Baptist Church on her account. But I don't care very much about that. You are a Presbyterian, and if you will only come and start a Presbyterian church, I will do everything for you that I say."

When the hour for dinner arrived, we two alone sat down to a table that fully redeemed the promise of the night before. We had as nice a turkey as ever tempted the appetite, and a superabundance of other dishes, "the best that the plantation afforded."

As I could only make a brief stay with my friend, I was anxious to leave something with him that would,

* This was, alas! too true—and true of a very large portion of country that I have visited, where the great majority of the preachers were uneducated.

if possible, deepen his religious impressions, and give him the instruction that he so much needed, after I had gone. Sitting at his bedside, I gave him Rev. Newman Hall's " Come to Jesus "—a few copies of which I usually carried in my saddle-bags. I expressed to him my very high appreciation of the little work, and, in order so to enlist his interest in it that he would not fail to read it after I had left him, I told him how very highly it was esteemed by the late General John H. Cocke, of Virginia, whom I had known some years before, while superintendent of the colporteur operations of the American Tract Society in that State. My host was of an old Virginia horse-racing, sporting family, and his pride in the old State insured his attention to anything I would say in regard to so distinguished a Virginian. So I proceeded :

" The General had a magnificent estate in Fluvanna County, Virginia—was President of the American Temperance Union, was prominently identified with many of our national benevolent institutions, and was withal very fond of doing good in a genial, quiet way. On one of his visits to Richmond, Miss Jennie Taylor, daughter of his old friend Rev. Dr. Taylor, of the Union Theological Seminary in Prince Edward County, had recently been married ; and, while attending to his business, he ran into the store of her husband to congratulate him. The bride was a great favorite with him, as she was with a very large circle of the best people in the State, who loved her for her own and her honored father's sake. As the General was about to leave, he said :

"'I wish to make you and your bride a very valuable present,' and handed him a tract of four pages.

"'Thank you,' said he, and immediately took from his desk a copy of 'Come to Jesus' and said, 'Please accept that in return, General, and don't fail to read it.'

"But a few days after this the General was in the city, and called again at the store, and said :

"'Where can I get copies of that little volume, "Come to Jesus"? I am delighted with it, and must have a quantity for distribution.'

"'I order them by the hundred copies from the Tract Society in New York,' was the response, 'and always keep a supply on hand to give away as I have opportunity.'

"The General soon procured a supply, and he had so many proofs of their great usefulness—so many of those to whom he gave them expressed their gratitude, and testified to the great benefit they had received from their perusal—that he ordered them again and again, and scattered hundreds of them over the country."

"How can I get a lot of them?" said my host, quite fired with the missionary spirit by this recital. I told him that I knew of no nearer place than the depository of the American Tract Society at Cincinnati, Ohio, which was several hundred miles distant. He would not rest until I had written out for him the address of Seely Wood, the depositary, and given him full instructions how to order them. On my next annual visit to the county I found several copies of "Come to Jesus" in the family of a Presbyterian elder, living near the county-seat, and, inquiring of him how he obtained them, he said:

"I· found a package of them addressed to me at the post-office, and the postmaster said they had been left there by Mr. —— " (my host), "and that he left several other packages there addressed to Rev. Mr. ——, principal of the seminary, and the officers of the different churches."

The matter was an inexplicable mystery to him, and to all that received those packages. They knew him well, and afterward described his character to me as far different from that which usually pertains to a tract-distributor. They told me that he was a very cruel master, and that it was the general belief that he had shot and secretly paid the owner his price for a negro because he thought him too intimate with his housekeeper.

At night I preached in a small schoolhouse, near his residence, to about a dozen persons who had assembled in response to the ringing of a small bell late in the afternoon and at the hour of assembling, the signal in all that region for preaching by a stranger, as I have elsewhere described.

Perhaps I should say that as a matter of form I asked my host, soon after my arrival, if he had received the letters I had forwarded to him, and sent his overseer's boys to school as he had proposed. He said he had received the letters, but gave some excuse or reason for not having sent them as yet. He ordered them dressed and called into the parlor for my inspection, that I might judge of their capacity for an education. This I afterward learned caused a great commotion in the "negro quarters," as they all thought I must be a "nigger-trader," and this examination was in reference to the price I would pay for them.

As my duties were very pressing, I spent but two nights with my host, and left him the next morning, with many thanks for his hospitality, and with earnest expressions of regret on his part—never to see him again.

A few months later I read a notice of his death in the papers, accompanied with this statement:

"He has left a very large estate. By his will he has freed a part of his slaves, and given his plantation and nearly all his property, including his slaves, to those he has freed."

On my next visit to the county seat, I hitched my horse to a post, and before entering any other house went directly to the county clerk's office and asked him

if he would do me the favor to allow me to read Mr.
——'s will. He at once produced the volume in which
it was recorded, and I was about to read it, when he
said:

"I have the original will here, if you would prefer
to see that."

I thanked him, and he handed it to me. It was in
his own handwriting. The spelling was very bad; as,
for instance, I remember that "be" was spelt "bea,"
and a good many other words were as badly spelled.
I have often been similarly astonished to find that men
who had a great deal of general intelligence, and were
most interesting talkers, were unable to spell the simplest sentence correctly. But the clerk told me that
he recorded the will exactly as it was written, and
that bad spelling did not vitiate any legal document.
The will was very brief, and I remember its principal
provisions as follows:

"I give and bequeath to ——" (the mother of his
children) "her liberty from the hour of my death."

"I give and bequeath to her children" (here followed the names of her five children) "their liberty
from the hour of my death."

"I give to ——" (another woman) "her liberty
from the hour of my death."

"I give to my brother —— my fiddle."

"I give to my brother —— my kitchen furniture."

These brothers, when visiting him, had in joke

asked him to make these legacies, saying that was all they wanted of his property, and he had *in earnest* told them he would give them what they asked. He also gave a little niece, the daughter of a sister, a valuable gold watch and chain, which he had promised her. He then gave a very small legacy—I think only three hundred dollars—to the mother of his children. Of her five children, only four were his. To these he gave all the remainder of his property, including plantation, blooded stock, slaves, money, etc., and directed that "they be sent to the State of New York," and placed in the best schools and thoroughly educated.*

Some ten days subsequent to the date of his will he had added a codicil. In this he gave the name and date of birth of each of the four children, in the order of their birth, and added, "These are my own children," and something like an appeal that they might be permitted to receive what he had left for them, and a hope that they might enjoy all that wealth and education could procure for them.

But the saddest, strangest thing about the will was its exceeding cruelty to the rest of his slaves. He directed that they all be sold for the benefit of his children that he had freed; and, that they might bring

---

* At the time of his death this property would have sold for nearly or quite a quarter of a million dollars. The plantation alone was sold under the hammer for ninety-five thousand dollars.

the greatest possible price, he ordered that they all be sent to New Orleans and sold upon the block at auction—not in families, but each one alone. His will directed his executor to advertise the "sale" for three months in the principal cities of the Southwest and South, so as to secure as large an attendance as possible of negro-traders and planters wishing to buy slaves. This horrified even his pro-slavery neighbors; for, had they been sold at home, many of them would have been bought by those who owned husbands and wives that were intermarried, or had "taken up" with them, and others would have been bought in the region, so that fewer families would have been separated. His own relatives, who would otherwise have inherited this large estate, were very wealthy, and he knew that they would spare no money in contesting his will. Hence he took precautions such as I have never heard of before to prevent its being broken. After he had got it written to suit himself—and I was told that he said he was inspired to write it—he made a large dinner-party, and among others invited the prominent physicians of the neighborhood. After the usual pleasures and excitements of such a party, as his guests were about leaving, he called the physicians to his room, and said:

"Gentlemen, you all know me well, and I wish to know if, from all that you have seen to-day, you think that I am competent to make my will?"

They all answered him in the affirmative. He then said, "I wish to know if this is your professional opinion, and that if called upon you will make oath to it?"

They again gave an affirmative response. He then took his will from his pocket, and said:

"Gentlemen, here is my will, written by myself, exactly as I want to dispose of my property, and I wish to sign it in your presence, and have you sign it as witnesses," which was done. Notwithstanding these precautions, I heard of the will as before the court, of the disagreement of the jury, and of the inability of the contestants to either establish or break it. I suppose the emancipation proclamation freed all the slaves before the case was settled by the courts. Fortunately for his children, I was told that he became so alarmed about them before he died, that he sent them to Ohio, and deposited money there for their support. Otherwise they would have remained slaves during the controversy in regard to the will. I have inquired after these children at Oberlin, at Xenia, and in many of the towns and cities of Ohio, but I have never been able to hear of them. I do not know whether or not they ever received the rest of the large estate which properly belonged to them.

I have written out these facts in all this detail, thinking that they would answer in part the query whether "anything strange or interesting did ever happen to a missionary," and also to reveal a type of character and civilization with which I have very often been brought in contact. I knew a free colored woman, and she was at the time a very liberal contributor to the American Bible Society, who told me that her own daughter had been educated at a fashionable. school by her white father, and was the wife of an officer in the United States Army. She visited her daughter frequently near one of the largest Northern cities, not as her mother, but as her old nurse or "mammy." Her husband supposed that her own brunette mother had died in her infancy, and that she had been "raised" by this "mammy," as such nurses were called, and hence their great affection for each other.

Within a few miles of the home of my host, in an adjoining county, I knew two colored girls whose mother was "as black as the hinges of midnight," whose white father and master had left them and a legacy for them in the care of a sister, to whom he had willed a large number of slaves; and those two girls were trained to call their mother "Margaret," and always to treat her as their "mammy." This was in anticipation of their going North to a fashionable boarding-school, and that their mother might gratify her maternal instincts by accompanying them or visiting them without detriment to their social standing or prospects. It was well known in the Southwest and South for many years before the war that, notwithstanding the intense prejudice on account of color so universal in the North, many of the most expensive and fashionable boarding-schools received pupils from Cuba, South America, and other tropical countries, even if their skins were decidedly dark. As colored children were so rigidly excluded from nearly all the best schools in the country, many availed themselves of the exception thus made in behalf of those of foreign birth by placing pupils in these schools whose tropical lineage was only "asserted" by those who paid their bills. A few Northern schools, as is well known, have always received colored pupils. Bishop Payne, of the African Methodist Episcopal Church, President of Wilberforce University, Xenia, Ohio, told me during the war that before the war most of his students were those who had been born slaves and were educated by their white fathers. The stories that they have communicated to him of the sufferings they have endured as they have thought of the life to which their children were exposed if left in slavery—and as they have traveled with them up the river, and been compelled to witness the indignities to which they were exposed, as they were obliged to leave them on deck with the rough crowds of passengers, liable at all times to the basest insults, while they, as they valued their lives, dared not offer them a father's protection—would alone make a volume of painfully thrilling interest. Alas, that there were many thousands of such parents whose natures were so blunted that they cared as little for their offspring as the dumb beasts around them!

But I have said all and more than I had intended, though very far from all that I could say upon this subject, and will betake myself to more pleasant and congenial narrations of my labors in the Brush.

SUPPLEMENTARY FACTS.

In writing the foregoing chapter, I, of deliberate purpose, suppressed the name and place of residence of the person whose remarkable history I have given in so much detail. I wished to make the case less personal than representative of a state of society now happily passed away. I gave the facts as far as I had received them.

But, since reaching New York, and while reading the proof-sheets of this volume, I have received additional facts from the highest authority; and, as the case has become so celebrated, there is now no reason why I should withhold any of them.

In the year 1859, one year after my election to the presidency of Cumberland College, I one day made a very long horseback-ride in order to reach the residence and spend the night with the Hon. Francis M. Bristow, at Elkton, Todd County, Kentucky. Mr. Bristow was at the time serving his second term as a member of Congress from the third district. I was anxious to see him, from the fact that, in accordance with instructions from the maker of the above-named will, the executor had employed him and his son, a young lawyer who had recently opened an office in Hopkinsville, Kentucky, to defend the will in a suit that had already been instituted in the Circuit Court. I did not find the distinguished Congressman at home, but was so fortunate as to meet and spend the night with his son.

I have called several times, since reaching the city, upon the "junior counsel for the will," now the Hon. Benjamin H. Bristow, late Secretary of the United States Treasury, Washington, D. C.

The maker of the will was Mr. Lycurgus B. Leavell, of Trenton, Todd County, Kentucky. General Bristow informs me that the case was tried before Hon. Thomas E. Dabney, at a term of the Circuit Court, held at Elkton, Kentucky. The senior counsel for the will was Hon. Francis M. Bristow; the junior counsel, Benjamin H. Bristow and H. G. Petrie. The senior counsel for the contestants was the Hon. Gustavus Henry, the "eagle orator" of Tennessee; the junior counsel was James E. Bailey, late United States Senator for Tennessee. As the case was so very important, the jury was selected from the most prominent and honorable slaveholders in the county. Young Bristow and Bailey opened the case. It was ably contested, and of most extraordinary interest, but this is not the place to describe it. The jury were eleven for and one against sustaining the will.

The war soon came on; the slaves, including several who had recently been imported from Africa in the Wanderer, were freed by the emancipation proclamation; the contest was withdrawn, and the will established. The executor and his bondsmen were financially ruined by the war, and only a small part of the estate, some forty thousand dollars, reached the two surviving children to whom it was devised. One of them, a young lady, has recently graduated with distinguished honor, and the president and professors of the college speak of her in terms of the very highest praise.

11

CHAPTER XIV

OLD-TIME ILLITERATE PREACHERS IN THE BRUSH.

I HAVE very often thought that the best work that could possibly be prepared in favor of an educated ministry, would be to send stenographers through those States where the census reveals the greatest amount of ignorance, to make *verbatim* reports of sermons that are actually preached, and publish them in a volume. Such a book would be the most remarkable exhibition of ignorance ever printed. Any one who has not traveled extensively will be astonished to learn of the great number of altogether unlearned and ignorant preachers who minister regularly to large congregations. I have found that the deeper I got into the Brush, and the denser the ignorance of the people, the greater was the number of preachers. I have seen a surprisingly large number of people who knew very little of the world, and a great deal less of books, to whom the honors of a preacher were very attractive. I say "honors," for the emoluments were so small that they had very little weight in the matter. I have known them to urge their own claims, and "electioneer" with others for years, and with the greatest pertinacity, in order to secure licensure and ordination. Some of them could not read at all, and many could read a verse or chapter only with the greatest difficulty, and miscalled a large number of the longer words.

I penetrated a wild region among the hills, and my own observations and the explorations that I caused to be made secured for it the undoubted and undesirable preëminence of being the banner county for ignorance and destitution of the Bible of all those that I visited. In some manner that I do not now remember, on my first visit I was directed to call upon one of the preachers of the county, who would coöperate with me in making arrangements to have it canvassed and supplied with the Bible. I found his house among the hills in the midst of a vast, dense forest, surrounded by a small clearing or "dead'ning," which was planted with corn and tobacco. He was rather a short, thickset man, with a powerful, muscular frame, and very quick and active in his movements. On riding up and introducing myself, he gave me a very cordial welcome to his home. It was a log-house, rather larger and higher than was usual in the region; but it was without chambers, and from floor to roof all was a single room. His family, including wife, mother-in-law, and children, numbered an even dozen. I spent the night with them, partaking of such food, using such knife, fork, and dishes, and occupying, with others, such a bed as I can not well describe, and I am sure my readers will not be able to imagine. But I had by this time become so accustomed to this kind of life in the Brush, that, if not pleasant and agreeable to me, it was at least not strange. Not long before, in a similarly wild region, in an adjoining county, I had slept in a much smaller cabin with one room, where the man and his wife and mother-in-law and four children, with another visitor besides myself, occupied three beds. I shared one of them, upon a very narrow bedstead, with the visitor, a neighbor who had called in for a social visit, as rough and tough-looking a long-haired backwoodsman as one often meets, dressed in butternut; and a "chunk of a boy," as his father called him, about a dozen years old, who was placed in the bed between us, with his head at our feet, and *ex necessitate* his feet not far from my head. It is a kind of lodging that can be endured for a night, as I know from positive experience. But I am not prepared to recommend it.

When I arrived at this house, which was about dinner-time, I found the children parching corn in a spider. The father was absent, and it was necessary for me to remain until he returned. The mother made no movements toward getting dinner, and said nothing about it, which was a very unusual thing in my experience. At length the children brought to me some of the corn, which was parched brown, but not popped. I had by this time become satisfied that this was to be their only dinner, and ate some of it with them. The father returned in a few hours, and urged me to spend the night with them, which in the circumstances I was glad to do; I could easily have gone farther and fared worse. He soon took a bag and went through the woods a mile or two to a neighbor's, and returned with some corn-meal and a piece of bacon. The entirely empty larder being thus replenished, a meal was soon cooked, and I sat down to what was to me both a dinner and supper of corn-dodger and fried bacon. I called upon some of the families in this neighborhood, and some months after met one of the young ladies at the county-seat. In talking with her in regard to this visit, I said:

"I was told that a number of the young women in your neighborhood can not read."

"Oh!" said she, "there are but two there that can read."

And yet I was told that there were two or three resident preachers there, but I had not time to call upon them. As the kind of food and lodging that I have described were so common to me, the chief "variety" that was the "spice" of my itinerant "life" was in the varied characters that I met. And I rarely found this "spice" of intenser flavor than in my own profession, among some of the preachers that I found in the Brush. The one that I had sought out, and with whose family I had spent the night, was one of the most remarkable of his type with whom I became acquainted.

In the morning he mounted his horse and rode with me to visit and confer with several of the leading citizens of the county in regard to its exploration, and to spend the following day, which was the Sabbath, in visiting two different and distant congregations, for the purpose of presenting the matter to them, and "lifting collections" in its aid. We rode several miles through the woods, only occasionally passing a small cabin and clearing, and made our first call at a log-house, where my clerical friend and guide was evidently a very great favorite. Here we were urged to have our horses put in the stable, and remain to dinner. We assented to this, and arrangements were at once made for convening a Bible committee, at a house in the neighborhood, that afternoon, and for religious services in the house at which we had stopped to dine that night. The husband and children at once started out to circulate these notices, and the wife began her preparations for our dinner. She was apparently about thirty years old, above the medium size, in a region of country where the most of the women were very large, with a bright, pleasant face, a cheerful, happy disposition, and very cordial and enthusiastic manners. The log-house, though not of the ' 't,

was decidedly of the better class; and our dinner, both
in its quality and the manner in which it was served,
was a great improvement upon my breakfast, and the
supper the night before. It was a happy group.
Conversation was cheerful and animated, and geniality
and joy glowed in all faces and pervaded all hearts.
Some time after dinner I started with my clerical friend
on foot through the woods to meet the Bible committee. After a pleasant interchange of views, we
appointed a colporteur to canvass the county, and adjourned. At once we received earnest invitations from
different ones to go home with them to supper. They
were unwilling that the family upon which we had
first called should monopolize the pleasure and honor
of entertaining us. I left my clerical friend to settle
this matter, and we went a mile or two in another
direction, where we were hospitably entertained at
supper. We then returned to the house where we
had dined, and it was soon filled with people, who
had assembled upon this brief notice. It was arranged
that instead of a sermon a chapter should be read, and
each of us should occupy a portion of the time in
brief addresses. My friend read the chapter. I was
astonished. I had never heard the like at any public religious service. Many of the words were mis-
pronounced and entirely miscalled, and it would have
been difficult to understand what was meant, from his
reading of the passage. But both his reading and re-

marks were very well received, and I saw no one who
seemed to notice that there was anything out of the
way with either. I followed him with some remarks,
and the meeting seemed to be greatly enjoyed by all.
Then began a very spirited contest as to where we
should go and spend the night. There were many
claimants for the honor.

"You must go home with me," said one.

"No," said another, "you had Brother A—— when
he was here, and you can't have these preachers. They
must go with me."

"No," said still another, "you've had the preachers a heap of times since I have. I hain't had nary
one in a long time, and they must go hum and stay
with me."

For myself, wearied as I was with the varied
labors of the day, I should have greatly preferred
remaining with the family where I was. But I left
the matter for them to decide, and we soon started
out, and taking a footpath through the underbrush,
among the large forest-trees, we went in the darkness
a mile or two, to an entirely new cabin. The logs
had been peeled, and it looked very clean and nice.
A large fire was soon blazing upon a hearth made of
fresh earth, and roaring up a chimney made of split
sticks covered with mud. It was the home of a young
couple, who had but recently married and commenced
housekeeping. There were two beds in the room.

We sat before the bright fire and talked for some time, until I told them how weary I was, and they pointed out the bed which the preacher and I were to occupy. The room was new and bright, and the sense of cleanliness was most grateful to my feelings. I thought that in that new house I should enjoy that rare luxury in the cabins in the Brush, a nice, untenanted bed and a pleasant sleep. As I turned down the blankets and moved my pillow to adjust it, I saw what I at first thought was a drop of molasses dried on the sheet. I impulsively moved my finger toward the spot to ascertain what it was, and it ran! My pleasant dreams were all banished, and I plunged in, in desperation, to share my bed with such company as for months and years I had found in so many of the log-houses in the Brush. The mild climate and the habits of the people conspired to make the beds quite too populous and repulsive to be described.

Though my meals were often such that only necessity compelled me to partake of them, yet the want of beds fit to be occupied by a human being, after my long, hard days' rides, was by far the greatest of all my privations and trials in the Brush. If I were to describe all that I have seen and endured in this matter, it would not only be very unpleasant and repulsive reading, but would surpass belief with all those not personally familiar with the country and the people described.

After breakfast the next morning we walked back to the house where we had first called and left our horses, and sat with the family until it was time to leave for church. As we sat together, my clerical friend, who was of an inquiring mind, turned to me and said, "How do you preach the first seven verses of the twelfth chapter of Ecclesiastes?"

I must here say that, in common with the great majority of his class, he used the word "preach" in the sense of "explain." My friend the Rev. Dr. S. H. Tyng, of New York, once told me that while preaching in a Southern State, in the early part of his ministry, a preacher of this class made him a visit. Seeing a pile of manuscripts upon his study-table, he inquired what they were, and was told that they were sermons.

"Why!" said he, in astonishment, "how many texts can you preach?"

These men were accustomed to "study" a passage in their manner, and form some opinions in regard to its meaning, and then they "preached" (explained) it on all occasions, with the most positive assurance in regard to the correctness of their views. Hence, when my friend asked me how I "preached" the passage alluded to, he wished from me a full exposition. Taking a Bible from the mantel-piece above the large fireplace, he turned to the chapter and read the first verse, as he had read the night before, and said to me, "How do you preach that?"

I gave my views of the passage in as few words as possible, and then he proceeded at much greater length to tell how he "preached" it.

As he concluded, the good sister, who had listened with face all aglow with delight, exclaimed : " Ah ! Brother P—— has studied *that!* "

In this manner he read, and we gave our views of each of the seven verses.

His "preach" was in each case much longer than mine, and invariably drew from the attentively listening sister the fervent expression of rapt admiration and delight: " Ah! Brother P—— has studied *that!* "

I am sorry that I can not tell my readers how he "preached" the entire passage; but it was so utterly strange, and so entirely unlike anything I had ever conceived of as possible to be said in explanation of this or any other passage of Scripture, that I confess I was obliged to exert myself to the utmost to maintain the gravity becoming my position. If I had smiled, I should have given great offense to the delighted sister, for no enthusiastic lady that I ever saw was more proud of her pastor than she was of her preacher at that moment. So earnest were my efforts to maintain my dignity, and not dishonor my exalted position as an agent of the American Bible Society, that I could not afterward recall his explanations but of two of the passages. I will give but one of them : " 'Or ever the silver cord be loosed.' The doctors

say that there is a cord that runs from the nape of
the neck, down the backbone, through the small of
the back, into the heart, right thar; and that when a
man dies that cord always snaps: that is the silver cord
loosed." (!)

"Ah!" said the sister, her face radiant with delight,
" Brother P—— has studied *that!* "

I will only add that this is a fair illustration of his
explanations of all the other verses. If I might mor-
alize upon this subject, I would repeat the opening
sentence of this chapter : "I have very often thought
that the best work that could possibly be prepared in
favor of an educated ministry, would be to send stenographers throughout the Brush, to make *verbatim*
reports of sermons that are actually preached, and publish them in a volume." Soon after this exposition,
we mounted our horses and attended services at two
different appointments, Brother P—— preaching at one
of them. About a year after this I saw him regularly
ordained to the full work of a minister of the gospel.

There are books containing " plans " or " skeletons "
of sermons, and some clergymen are said to make free
use of them in the preparation of their sermons. I will
give one which may aid some limping preacher who
needs such helps, and hereby offer it as a contribution to
the next volume of skeleton sermons that may be com-
piled. The sermon was preached to quite a large congregation in a grove, where I was present and occupied

the "stand" with the preacher. His text was Job xxvi, 14: "Lo, these are parts of his ways: but how little a portion is heard of him? but the thunder of his power who can understand?" After an introduction that was quite as appropriate to any other verse in the Bible as to this, the preacher said:

"In further discoursing upon this passage, I shall, in the first place, review the chapter, and show what is meant by the word 'these.' I shall, in the second place, mention some of the works of God. I shall, in the third place, conclude, according to circumstances, light and liberty being given."

I must say to my readers, in explanation of his "third place," that the "plan" and effort in sermons, addresses to juries, political and all other speeches in the Southwest, was to wind up with as grand and stirring a conclusion as possible. Here the congregation was to be deeply moved, the jury to be melted, and the crowd to demonstrate by their applause how they would vote. These perorations often reminded me of the manner in which the stage-coaches of the olden time used to drive into my native village, in the days of my boyhood; when the driver cracked his long whip, blew stirring blasts from his tin horn, and his four horses rushed up to the village tavern on the jump, his noisy demonstrations startling all the villagers. It was so with these sermons and speeches. However lame and limping in their progress, there was always, if possible, a rousing conclusion, a demonstrative drive into town. Hence, my clerical friend did not wish to embarrass himself by announcing definitely what he would say in his conclusion; but left himself free to soar and roar "according to circumstances, light and liberty being given." He went through with his sermon according to his "plan," but his conclusion did not arouse and move his audience like many that I have heard.

I have already spoken of the genial friend to whom I sold my faithful horse, and of the accounts that he gave me of the preachers he had known and the preaching he had heard. He told me that upon one occasion he heard the funeral sermon of a child preached from the text, "Write, Blessed are the dead," etc. The preacher was so ignorant in regard to spelling that he supposed the "write" in the text was "right," not wrong, and he endeavored to comfort the parents by showing them that it was "right" that people should suffer affliction, "right" that their children should sicken and die, and that all the Lord's dealings with his people were "right."

On another occasion he attended a meeting where a number of ministers were present, and the opening sermon was preached by an old acquaintance and friend, who owned a good plantation, a number of slaves, and for many years preached regularly on alternate Sabbaths to two quite large congregations. There are many thousands of people who rarely, if ever, hear a sermon from an educated minister. These people have strong and well-defined notions as to the kind of preaching that suits them. If the preacher ranges extensively over the Bible, and quotes a great deal of Scripture without any regard to its appropriateness or connection with the text, they say of him approvingly: "He's a Scripter preacher. He's not a larnt man, but he's a real Scripter preacher." Hence, many of these preachers range over both the Old and New Testaments in every sermon, and quote as much as they can, with as little connection as a page in the dictionary.

The preacher on this occasion took for his text the words: "The name of the Lord is a strong tower; the righteous runneth into it, and is safe." He described these towers as places of safety, ranged through the Old Testament, and, coming down to the New, said: "The world was then in an awful condition; there were no towers, no places of safety! The whole generation was without a tower! You may say: 'How do you know this is so? You haven't much learning. You haven't read many histories.' Ah! but I've got Scripter for it. I don't want any histories when I've got the Bible for it. Here it is. Peter, preaching to them on the day of Pentecost, said, 'Save yourselves from this untowered generation.'"

After the meeting "broke," and they mounted their horses to ride to dinner, my old friend said to the preacher:

"Why, Brother Mansfield, you made a great mistake in your sermon this morning."

" Mistake !" said he, "what was it, Brother Roach ?"

" Why, that about the ' untowered generation.' It is not untowered," said he ; "it is untoward. It is, ' Save yourselves from this untoward generation.' "

The preacher dropped his head, thought a moment, and then said :

"There can't be any mistake about that. Why, I've preached it that way more than a dozen times."

When they reached the house where they were to dine, they found a dictionary, and that was appealed to to settle the matter. Alas, that the verdict spoiled a favorite sermon!

I was about as much astonished at the facts I heard in regard to the salaries that were paid to these preachers, with all the formalities of a regular contract, as at anything I ever learned in regard to their preaching. I once occupied the pulpit with one of them, in a church which was a large, barn-like brick structure, having four doors, one near each corner, for the ingress and egress of the congregation. This preacher was a great favorite in the region, with both the white and colored people, and was familiarly known as "Jimmy B——." He had stentorian lungs, was wonderfully voluble, and his sing-song "holy tone" was most delightful to his audience. It was a warm summer day, and the house was packed with whites dressed in butternut jeans, and groups of colored people were standing outside near each open window. It was a monthly service, and all seemed to enjoy it greatly.

In the afternoon, after the custom of the Southwest, he preached to the "servants," and I again occupied a seat in the pulpit with him. His colored audience was moved by his stentorian voice and avalanche of words to the extremest excitement and joy. At the conclusion of his sermon they could not separate without singing some of their "breaking" songs, and all marching by the pulpit and shaking hands with the preachers. This hand-shaking was one of the most marked features of their religious services, and these "breaking" or parting exercises have afforded me the opportunity of hearing the grandest, wildest, most beautiful and genuine African melodies to which I have ever listened. As I was a "visiting brother," I was entitled to as warm and cordial a greeting as the one who had preached. The leader commenced a hymn familiar to the large audience, and they began to sing and move in procession by the low pulpit where we were standing, shaking hands with each of us as they passed. As the long procession filed by, their dark faces shining with delight, the music arose louder, wilder, and more exciting, until they seemed entirely unconscious of the strength of the grip they gave my poor, suffering hand. I was unwilling to mar their joy by withdrawing it altogether, and, to save it from being utterly crushed, I resorted to the expedient of suddenly clutching the end of the fingers of each hand that was extended to me by the excited and happy singers, and so they were unable to give me their vise-like squeeze, and I escaped comparatively unharmed. The hand-shaking ended, the meeting "broke," and they all dispersed, masters and slaves highly delighted with the preacher and all the services of the day.

My host upon this occasion was the hotel-keeper of the place. In talking with him about the great popularity of this preacher, he said that, if equally extended notice should be given that he would preach there on one Sabbath, and the Rev. Dr. Young, the learned and eloquent President of the college at Danville, would preach there on another, Jimmy B—— would call together the largest audience. At another place, when quite a number of persons were present, reference was made to the salary that was received by this popular favorite. I made particular inquiries upon this subject, and learned that the church negotiated with him to preach for them one Sabbath each month during the year, for one dollar a Sabbath. Hence, they paid him twelve dollars a year for one fourth of his time. Some of them thought that as neither he nor any other good hand could at that time get more than fifty cents a day for mauling rails, hoeing corn, or any other labor, this salary was rather excessive; but in consideration of the fact that he had to leave home on Saturday evening in order to meet his appointment, and furnish his own riding-nag, they magnanimously voted him the full dollar a Sunday, "for one fourth of his time." I was informed that he preached to other churches, but did not learn that any of them paid him a larger salary. In another place that I visited, the Rev. James L——had preached to the same church twenty-one years, and he said the largest sum he had ever received for preaching in any one year was twenty dollars, and he had often received less than ten dollars! Very many of these churches were entirely satisfied if they had regular preaching once a month. In riding through the Brush, I used often to gratify my curiosity by making inquiries in regard to the salaries received by those who preached in the churches that I passed. Once, in riding late in the evening, I overtook—or, in the vernacular of the region, "met up with"—a boy some twelve or fourteen years old, who was riding a mule. After exchanging "howd'ys," I found him very loquacious, and disposed to enlighten me in regard to everything in the neighborhood. I asked him what salary they paid their preacher. "Oh!" said he, "they pay the one they have got now right smart. They give him a dollar and a half a Sunday."

We passed a church where the members washed one another's feet at each communion. I made some inquiries in regard to the ceremony, and he told me the brethren washed only the brethren's feet, and the sisters the sisters' feet. I told him that I supposed they only sprinkled water upon their feet—they did not wash much. "Oh!" said he, "sometimes they gets happy, and washes right hard." I had spent a Sabbath at a meeting in the woods with the poet of this denomination, and purchased of him a hymn-book that he had been duly authorized to compile and publish for them, containing some hymns that he had written to be sung at these feet-washing services. He was one of the most illiterate men I ever met. I regret to say that I have lost the book, and can not transcribe some of these original hymns for the benefit of my readers. I had a good deal of conversation with this "poet," and he told me he was at the time engaged in teaching school. I afterward met the school commissioner, a lawyer, at the county-seat, who had examined him and given him his license to teach, and rallied him jocosely for giving a man that was so ignorant, authority to teach a public school.

"Oh!" said he, "I only certified that he was competent to teach *in that neighborhood.*"

For years I was accustomed to avail myself of every opportunity of hearing these illiterate preachers, both white and colored, consistent with my other duties. It was a new and interesting study to me. Sometimes I got rare kernels of wheat in the midst of a great deal of chaff, rich nuggets of gold among a great deal of sand and rubbish; and I always felt more than repaid for the time thus expended. It was interesting to observe the workings of minds, often of superior natural powers, in their attempts to elucidate the Scriptures. It was especially strange to hear them render any Scripture narrative, entirely in their own Brush vernacular. I have often regretted that I did not take down many of these narratives of Bible facts at the time I heard them. But the unusual sight of a person thus employed in a congregation would attract more attention than the preacher himself, and I was therefore unwilling to do it. But I can give my readers a very correct idea of these narratives.

In riding through a very rough, wild region, I fell in company with a gentleman on horseback, and rode some distance with him. He told me that a preacher, who was so illiterate that it was with the greatest difficulty that he could study out a chapter in the Bible, sometimes preached in a log schoolhouse in his neighborhood, and he had heard him the Sabbath before. It was in a region where a rough-and-tumble fight would attract more attention than anything else. The preacher had a theme of the deepest interest to himself and the most of his congregation. This gentleman gave me quite a full outline of the discourse, and I write it out from his description, and fill it up as my extended acquaintance with these people, and knowledge of their vernacular, derived from years of constant mingling with them, enable me to do.

"Last week, my breethrin, as I was a-readin' my Bible, I found a story of a big fight (1 Samuel, xvii). It was powerful interestin', and I studied it 'most all the week. There was two armies campin' on two mountains right fornenst each other; and a holler and, I reckon, some good bottom-land and a medder-lot lying between 'em. In one of the armies there was a big feller—a whoppin', great, big feller—and every day he went down into the medder-lot and looked up the hill to t'other camp, and jest dared 'em! He told 'em to pick their best man and send him down, and he'd fight him. And he jest strutted around there in his soger-close, and waited for 'em to send on their man. And such soger-close I never heerd tell on afore. He had a brass cap and brass trousers, and a coat made like mail-bags where they are all ironed and riveted together. But the fellers in t'other camp just clean flunked. They darn't fight the big feller, nary one of 'em. They jest all sneaked away, and the big feller he went back to camp. But he didn't quit thar, the big feller didn't. He was spilin' for a fight, and he was bound to have it. He jest went down into the bottom-land, into the medder-lot, every day, mornin' and evenin', and dared 'em and dared 'em. I tell you he did pester 'em mightily. The old feller, Saul, the gineral, he felt more chawed up and meaner than the sogers, and, when he couldn't stan' it no longer, he told the boys if any of 'em would

go down and lick that big feller he'd give him his
gal, and a right smart chance of plunder. But they
was all so skeer'd that even that didn't start one of
'em. The big feller went down and dared 'em and
pestered 'em more'n a month—forty days, the Bible
says. I don't know what they'd a-done if it hadn't a-
be'n that a peart little feller had come down to camp
one day to fetch some extra rations to his three big
brothers. that their old dad had sent to 'em from
home. Kind old pap he was, and sharp, too, for he
sent along a big present to the boys' cap'en. Well,
jest as little brother drove up, they was all gwine
out to fight, and the little feller left his traps with
the driver, legged it after the sogers, and told his
big brothers howd'y. Right thar the old big feller
come out and dared 'em agin, and they was all so
skeer'd that they jest run like mad. The little feller
heerd him, and then went back into camp and heerd
all the sogers talking about him, and what the old
gineral would give to have him licked. He asked
'em a heap of questions about it all, and big brother
he got mad at him, and twitted him about keeping
sheep, and give him a right smart of sass. He was
plucky, but you see he had to stan' it, 'cause 'twas
big brother. Big brothers are mighty mean sometimes.

"But the little feller talked a heap with the other
sogers, and they told the old gineral about him, and
he told them to tell the little feller to come and see

him. The little feller was mighty plucky, and he jest
up and told the old Gineral Saul that *he'd fight the
big feller!* The gineral looked at the handsome little
feller—he was raal handsome—and ses he, kinder soft-
ly, I reckon, and shakin' his head : 'It's too big a job;
you're only a chunk of a boy, and he's an old fighter.'
The little feller spunked up and told the old gineral
that he'd had one b'ar-fight, and he'd killed the b'ar.
He said there was an old lion and a b'ar got among
his dad's sheep, and was gwine off with a lamb. He
broke for 'im, and as soon as he met up with the old
b'ar he lamm'd him, till the b'ar turned on him for a
hug; but he got one hand into the long ha'r, under
his jaw, and he lamm'd him with the other till he was
dead. He'd killed the lion and the b'ar, and he know'd
he was enough for the old big feller.

"Then the little feller talked raal religious to the
old gineral. You see he'd got religion afore that, and
he know'd that the Lord would help a feller, if he was
all right, and got in a tight place. He told Gineral
Saul that the Lord had made him mighty supple, and
looked out for him when the old lion and b'ar tried
to get their paws into him ; and he knew he'd see him
through the fight with the old big feller; for *he* was
jest darin' 'em and pesterin' 'em to make game of religion. When the old gineral seed he was so plucky,
and religious too, he know'd them's the kind that fit
powerful, and he told him to go in, and he made a

little pra'r for him hisself. Then the old gineral put his own soger-close on the little feller, and strapped his sword on to him. But they was all a heap too big, and he shucked 'em off d'rectly, and made for a dry branch down in the bottom. There he hunted five little rocks, smooth as a hen-egg, put 'em in a little bag where he carried his snack when he was a-tendin' the sheep, got his sling fixed all right, and hurried up to meet the old big feller in the medder-lot. When he seed him comin' he was powerful mad they'd sent down such a little feller, and jawed awful. But the little feller jest talked back religious, and kept his eye peeled. And I *reckon* the big feller couldn't a be'n a lookin'. I've studied a heap on it, and I jest know the big feller couldn't a-be'n a-lookin'; for the little feller got out his sling, and drew away, and shied a little rock at him, and he popped him, and down he tumbled. Then the little feller rushed up and mounted on him, jest as an old hunter loves to get on a b'ar after he's shot him; and he out with the big feller's long sword and off with his head. Then it was them Philistine sinners' turn to be skeer'd, and they broke for the brush; and all them chil'en of Israel fellers jest shouted and chased 'em clean over the mountain into a valley, and then com'd back and got all their camp-plunder.

"My breethrin, that's the best story of a fight I ever read after; and you can't buy no better story-book than this 'ere Bible."

12

If the facts presented in this chapter make a draft on the credence of any of my readers that they find it difficult to honor, I respectfully commend to them the study of the late United States census, especially its portrayal of the illiteracy of the late slave States. The figures are as humiliating as they are startling. They seem at length to be forcing themselves upon the attention of the President, Congress, and the country. But no figures can ever make any such impression as the actual personal contact I have had with thousands of these people in their own homes, since the commencement of my labors among them in 1843.

But my account of " Old-Time Illiterate Preachers in the Southwest" would be very incomplete if it did not include some of the notable

NEGRO PREACHERS OF THE OLD RÉGIME.

I used to take great interest in hearing them preach, and availed myself of every possible opportunity to do so, consistent with my duties. Many of these preachers were very devout and godly men. They had good judgment, strong native sense, and exerted a great influence over the slaves, which was highly appreciated by their masters. They also gratified in a measure the religious instincts of the slaves, by officiating at their weddings and funerals.

One of the largest, most orderly, and impressive

funeral processions that I have ever witnessed, was that of an old negro preacher at Lexington, Kentucky, who had been the pastor of a large colored church in that city for many years. It was upon a Sabbath afternoon, during a meeting of the Synod of Kentucky, which I was attending. Hundreds of slaves came in from the surrounding country, and it was estimated that there were from two to three thousand in the procession. Nearly every family-carriage in the city and the surrounding country was in the line, occupied by the " family servants." These carriages were sent by the owners, as their tribute to the old preacher for his great and good influence over their slaves. The most of the men marched some four or six abreast, with slow and solemn tread, and that silent awe to which their natures are so susceptible in the presence of death.

I knew another negro preacher, and often heard him address his people, for whom I had the profoundest respect. He was a devout and saintly man, and his dignified port and bearing were those of a born gentleman. He was often engaged the whole week "attending masons." I have often met him as he was driving a horse, sitting upon a wagon-load of mortar, thoroughly bespattered, and received from him a bow so easy, dignified, and graceful, that many a Governor and Congressman that I have known might well covet his distinguished bearing.

Upon one occasion I heard him preach a sermon to

his congregation, enforcing the duty of keeping their hearts pure and free from all evil thoughts, when he abruptly broke forth: " But you say, ' I can't, I can't. These bad thoughts come to me, and I can't help it.' I know you can't help it," said he, " and I know, too, that you can't help the birds flying over your heads; but you can help their building nests in your ha'r " (hair).

The public political, theological, and other discussions, that I have already described in this volume, developed a love of religious controversy in the Southwest such as I have never known among any other people.

The negroes were echoes and imitators of the whites in this respect as in others. Morning services were for the white congregations, but slaves usually attended them, often in large numbers. The afternoons were mostly given up to the colored people, and they were free to attend religious services, whether they were ministered to by white or negro preachers. If there was a public discussion, or any special interest or excitement upon any subject at the morning service, that was almost certain to be the theme of the negro preacher's discourse to his afternoon audience.

The overwhelming majority of colored church-members were either Baptists or Methodists. The differences of these churches in doctrinal belief were the theme of almost endless controversy between the colored champions and defenders of these opposing creeds.

Some of these discussions were original and spicy, beyond anything I have ever heard of in the line of theological controversy. I will give a few characteristic illustrations.

I had preached in the morning at a small county-seat village, and after dinner set out, with a venerable and estimable Methodist "local preacher," to attend his afternoon appointment. After a ride of several miles, we reached the brow of a very deep and narrow ravine, which we were to cross. At the moment of our arrival a venerable, gray-haired black man, mounted upon a fine horse, appeared upon the opposite brow. At the first sight of him I turned to my companion and said:

"That must be a brother preacher."

"Oh, yes," said he, "he is a very distinguished preacher. He is the champion and defender of the Methodist Church among the colored people in all this region. He is an old and favorite family servant, and his master, who is a graduate of West Point, allows him to use that fine horse in going to his afternoon appointments."

As we passed him, he returned "the bow professional" with a dignity and a Methodistic swing that would have done honor to such old itinerants as Bishop Asbury and Bishop Soule. Such was my first acquaintance with the Rev. Nathan Board, whose controversial exploits I am about to relate. As we rode on, my friend informed me that upon one occasion, when Nathan was present at a Baptist church at a communion, the preacher, in giving the reason why they did not invite those of other denominations who were present to commune with them, said :

"We are not alone and singular in the fact that we do not invite you all to commune with us. Presbyterians fence the tables. Methodists fence the tables. All other denominations fence the tables. They do not allow anybody and everybody to commune with them. We all fence the tables. The only difference is, that the Baptist fence is a little higher than any of the others."

In the afternoon Nathan preached to his people, and as some of them had been present in the morning and heard this address, he had to answer it for their benefit. After repeating the whole address, he said :

"Now, my bruddren, I'd rather have a low fence and a tight one, than a high fence and a good many holes in it."

As these Baptists were of the anti-mission class, who opposed an educated and paid ministry, Sabbath-schools, Bible societies, and all mission enterprises, but favored good Bourbon, Nathan's reply was regarded as decidedly personal, and some of them thought he ought to be "whooped" (whipped) for his impudence.

A few weeks after this I reached a county-seat village upon the Ohio River, and learned that it had recently been the theatre of a very exciting theological controversy among the slaves.

A colored Baptist preacher, of great reputation among his brethren for boldness and polemical skill as the champion and defender of his denomination, a Calvinist of the stern John Knox order, became greatly excited on account of what he esteemed the heretical doctrines and bad influence of Methodism. After mature deliberation, he determined that he would wage against it a war of extermination in the community.

Having formed this resolution, for successive Sabbaths he labored in the work, and discharged his batteries with most telling effect. His victory was a signal one. Arminianism was overwhelmed—the Methodists were completely routed. They had no preacher that they dared to put up to answer their opponent, and they could only manfully acknowledge that they were beaten for the present, and adjourn their defense to some future day. I was only able to learn the manner in which he discussed the antagonistic Arminian and Calvinistic doctrines of "falling from grace," and the "perseverance of the saints." But, if that was a specimen of the entire discussion, any one at all acquainted with slave preaching, with the frequent use made by these preachers of *illustrations* and *comparisons*, and the great effects produced by them upon the minds of the slaves, can well understand how this preacher had such power over his audience. It was as follows :

" De Methodiss, my bruddren, is like de grasshopper—hoppin', all de time hoppin'—hop into heaven, hop out, hop into heaven, hop out. But, my bruddren, de Baptiss, when he get to heaven, *he's dar!* De Baptiss is like de 'possum. Hunter get after him, he climb de tree; he shake de limb, one foot gone; he shake de limb, anudder foot gone; he shake de limb, ebbery foot gone; but tink you, my bruddren, *'possum fall?* You know, my bruddren—you cotch too many —you know *'possum hang on by de tail,* and de berry debbil can't shake him off!"

The head Methodists, after many conferences, concluded that they would make one desperate effort to save their cause. After discussing the merits of all their preachers far and near, they decided to send for the Rev. Nathan Board, the veteran war-horse in theological polemics I have already introduced to my readers. This venerable preacher of the olden time was a genuine African, and entered his profession before it was fashionable for those of his class to learn to read; but he had a strong memory, which made up somewhat for this "defect" in his education, and, if he could not remember the very thing that he wished to repeat, he could always remember *something;* and, therefore, he was never at a loss for a quotation from Scripture, or an illustration.

The appointed Sabbath arrived, and Nathan was on the ground. The intense excitement among the blacks had aroused the curiosity of the whites, and there was a general turnout of white and black to hear Nathan's defense. His brethren had in private gone over all the strong points that had been made by their opponent, had given him a graphic and glowing picture of the utterly prostrate condition of their cause, and with the eloquence of the deepest feeling had endeavored to impress him with the magnitude of the interests involved in his success or failure. Nathan was greatly excited, but he was confident of his ability to meet the emergency. He had not read books, but in the previous fifty years he had witnessed many a fierce and bitter contest between successive Governors, Congressmen, and others, in their hot race for office, and his polemical tastes had made him a close observer of the various methods of meeting and overwhelming an opponent. That my readers may understand what follows, I must premise that the American Bible Union, under the presidency of the Rev. Spencer H. Cone, D. D., was at the time very earnestly engaged in the revision of the Bible; that the Baptist churches in the Southwest very generally coöperated in this work; that pastors of churches and agents of the society were urging its necessity, and soliciting collections in its aid; and that the other denominations were very generally defending King James's translation, and opposing the new version. Hence the question was the subject of almost universal discussion by the white clergymen; and, as I have already said, the colored preachers were but their echoes—they all felt called upon to enlighten their congregations upon this, as upon all other questions.

Having gone through the preliminary services, Nathan arose and commenced his sermon as follows:

"My bruddren, I has been sent for to come here and preach, and, when I gets t'rough, you'll t'ink I *has* preached. You'll find my text, if my memory sarve me, in de book of de Revolution: 'For de great day of his raff is come, and who do you t'ink is gwine to stand?'"

Nathan was too full to spend any time in introduction. He broke out at once, in the most emphatic manner: "And do you t'ink, my bruddren, de Baptiss will den be able to stand?" Shutting his eyes and shaking his head most dubiously, with his peculiar guttural "Umph! ah! my Lord! and you'll see 'em paddling den. All de water in de Ohio River won't save 'em den; dey'll call for de rocks and de mountains to fall on 'em in dat great day of his *raff*, and I'll tell you, my bruddren, dat a hot rock will be a mighty tight place for a Baptiss."

Having thus given vent to his feelings, in imitation of Cicero's immortal philippic against Catiline, he proceeded with more deliberation and at great length to review the entire ground that had been traveled over by his theological assailant.

The grasshopper, the 'possum, and all the other strong points were taken up and disposed of to the entire satisfaction of his brethren. The stunning blows that he had dealt in his opening passage were followed by others, scarcely less telling, all the way through to the peroration. Already he saw in the faces of his audience undoubted evidence of the success of his efforts, and he was flushed with victory. His tone became triumphant, if not overbearing. His bitterness and severity would surely have been entirely inexcusable, but for the excitement he was under from the terrible provocation. That " grasshopper " comparison was the most damaging assault upon Methodism, the most crushing blow to Arminianism, that he had ever been called upon to repel, in all the long years of his ministry. That of itself was enough to fire all the blood of this old theological war-horse. And then to follow that with the "'possum"--that was the crowning indignity—that was a Calvinistic blow administered to an already crushed and fallen foe, which Nathan's Arminian blood was fired to punish to the very utmost extent of his power. In Nathan's intense admiration for his Master he had, with the extraordinary imitative powers of his race, taken on, in addition to the clerical, a very decided military bearing. In his composite character, he represented the dignity of the bishop and the boldness and dash of the successful general. He was, therefore, a very striking representative of the " church militant," and he put into the remainder of his defense the concentrated polemical power of the two professions. He proceeded:

"De Baptiss, my bruddren, is in such a gone case, dey is in such a mighty tight fix, dat de ole Bible—de Bible dat all de faders and mudders have gone to heaven wid—de Bible dat dey used to love such a heap—de ole Bible dat fill us wid de hebbenly fire all de way along de road to Canaan—dat ole Bible, my bruddren, is no account any more to de Baptiss, and dey say dat the Baptiss is a gwine to get up a new deversion. In de ole Bible it reads, if my memory sarve me, 'In dose days came John de Baptiss.' Dey say in de new deversion its gwine to read, 'In dose days came John de Immerser'—'tain't dar, my bruddren. In de ole Bible it reads, if my memory sarve me, 'He shall baptize you wid de Holy Ghost and wid de fire.' Dey say dat in de new deversion it's gwine to read, 'He shall *immerse* you wid de Holy Ghost and wid de fire'—'tain't dar, my bruddren! Immersin' wid fire, my bruddren!—immersin' wid fire! Who ever read in de Bible 'bout immersin' wid fire, *only* dem chil'en of de three Hebrewsers? Dey was immersed wid fire —dem three Hebrewsers dat was put into de furnace, heated seven times hot by de dedict of Nebuckefalus —what you call 'em now" (scratching his head)— "Shamrack, Shimshack, and Bedgone. Dey ar all dat we read in de Bible 'bout bein' immersed wid fire."

This was the finishing blow. Nathan sat down. The excitement and joy of his brethren were unbounded. They shouted, danced, shook hands, hugged, and yielded themselves up to that perfect luxury of excited, joyous feeling of which they alone seem capable.

My esteemed friend the late Rev. W. W. Hill, D. D., to whom my readers are indebted for the story of the candidate and his Greek quotations, gave me the following facts, illustrating the argumentative power of an old-time slave preacher:

At the commencement of the Doctor's ministry he was for several years the pastor of a church that had been founded in the early history of the State, and ministered to for a lifetime by a distinguished Scotch minister. He had indoctrinated the entire community, and built up a very strong Presbyterian church. Dr. Hill, who was a native of the State, and greatly interested in the colored people, was very often invited to preach to a colored Baptist church in the afternoon, which he always did with the greatest pleasure. It is perhaps not known to all my readers that the slaves always assumed and stoutly maintained among themselves the relative social rank and position of their masters. If the master was a President, Governor, Member of Congress, Judge, or a man of large wealth, all his slaves participated in his honors, and often bore them more conspicuously and proudly than he did.

It so happened that in Dr. Hill's congregation the families of highest social position were Presbyterians. Some of the slaves, quite naturally for them, got the impression that the Presbyterian Church was " de 'ristocratic church," and thought it would be a nice thing if they could have a Presbyterian church for the colored people. But they were all thoroughly indoctrinated in the Baptist creed—and there was the rub. " Christ went down *into* the water, and came up *out* of the water." That, in their minds, was the hard thing to be overcome. But the desire to attain social elevation through church relations has often caused other than colored people to make extraordinary struggles, and they were willing to put forth the effort. After many conferences upon the subject among themselves, they concluded to invite Dr. Hill to preach on the subject of baptism, and explain and defend the Presbyterian views. They accordingly called on him, and presented their request, which surprised him very much. He said to them :

" I have preached for you, whenever you have invited me, for several years, and you all know that I have never said one word upon the subject of baptism. I do not like to do it now. The people will not understand it, and will think I am trying to proselyte you."

But they told him that they had been appointed a committee to invite him to preach on the subject, and that it would be understood by all that he preached on baptism at their request. Upon this statement he accepted the invitation and afterward preached for them as requested. But his effort was a decided failure; he did not "move de difficulties." "Christ went down *into* the water, and came up *out* of the water." That was still the great stumbling-block in the way of the organization of a Presbyterian church for the colored people. Some weeks afterward Judge Green, of Danville, Kentucky, drove over in his family carriage to make a visit and spend a Sabbath with some of his friends in this congregation.

It soon became noised abroad among the slaves that the *driver* of this distinguished jurist was not only, like his master, a Presbyterian, but he was a noted Presbyterian preacher.*

The committee who had invited Dr. Hill to make the effort that proved so unsuccessful, at once waited upon their distinguished visitor, and invited him to preach to them upon the subject of baptism. He was from Danville, the seat of a Presbyterian college, the Jerusalem of the Presbyterian Church in Kentucky. Hence the honor of that Church among the colored people of that State was largely in his keeping, and he appreciated his responsibilities. He accepted the invitation promptly, and, like the Rev. Nathan Board,

---

* I do not know that I need to say that these slave preachers were not regularly licensed and ordained by any ecclesiastical body. They simply assumed the profession, and were recognized as preachers among their own people.

he was confident and eager to stand forth as the champion of his church. He was greeted with a large congregation, and his effort was a decided success.

Some days after, Dr. Hill met some of the committee, and said to them:

"I understand that this colored Presbyterian minister from Danville preached on baptism last Sunday, and that he has made the whole matter entirely clear and satisfactory to you all."

They assured him that that was true.

"Now," said the Doctor, "that seems very strange to me. You all profess to like my preaching, and are generally full of compliments and thanks for my sermons. I have done my very best for you on this subject of baptism. I have told you all I know—all I have learned from Hebrew and Greek—and it did not do one bit of good. And now this colored minister from Danville preaches to you, and beats me entirely. He makes the whole subject plain and satisfactory to you. Can you tell me what he said?"

"Oh, yes, yes, yes!" they responded. "His tex' was, 'My sheep hears my voice, and I knows them, and dey follows me.' Den he said, 'In de Bible de Christians is de sheep.' He had a heap of Bible on dat p'int, and he preached a mighty long time and make dat so strong, no nigger can't 'spute it. And den he said, mighty strong, 'Now, my bruddren and sisters, you all knows you can't get a sheep into de wa-

ter nohow, 'less you cotch him and carries him in.'
And, preacher, you knows dat is so yourself."

I give these truthful sketches of old-time slave preachers and preaching in the hope that others may follow my example, and preserve as many as possible of these illustrations of a state of things now rapidly passing away, through the labors of an educated ministry.

CHAPTER XV.

"ORTONVILLE"; OR, THE UNIVERSAL POWER OF SACRED
SONG.

I HAVE a distinct recollection of the circumstances
of my first acquaintance with "Ortonville," a piece of
sacred music by the late Professor Thomas Hastings.
It was more than forty years ago. The church choir
in my native place, a small country village in western
New York, had gone down to that sad pass, that for
several Sabbaths the alternative was either to have no
singing at all, or a maiden lady, a veteran member of
the choir, must "pitch the tune." This, even in the
estimation of the most staid and least nervous of the
congregation, was quite too bad; and the matter was
taken up and talked over in earnest at the village store,
where all matters public and private pertaining to the
neighborhood and town were discussed, and public sentiment on all questions was regulated, like the price of
stocks at a board of brokers. The result of this discussion was, that a subscription-paper was started, and a

singing-master employed for one evening each week during the winter, who, according to immemorial custom, was paid three dollars an evening for his services, and the school was free to all who were disposed to attend.

A country singing-school — who, that has ever attended one, is not carried back to some of the most delightful scenes of his earlier years by the mere mention of the name? What visions of early playmates and schoolmates, of bright moonlight rides, with the merry chimes of bells and shouts of joyous hearts, as group after group from different families was gathered for the school, and crowded into the capacious sleigh— mothers' warm, home-made mittens, stockings, and flannels, and all the buffalo-robes in the neighborhood, bidding defiance to an atmosphere at zero! And then the frank, unstudied greetings and companionship at the village church; the lighting of candles that each one had brought from home (no lamps or sextons in those days); the first essays, of each pupil alone, at the ascending and descending scale, with this one's failure and that one's success; the coquettings and rivalries of the "intermission," and the successful and unsuccessful offers of the youthful beaux to "go home with the girls" at the close of the school—these and a thousand other pleasant memories come thronging upon the mind at the remembrance of a country singing-school!

We had spent several evenings upon the rudiments, singing from the blackboard; the teacher had decided that the old books would not do (what singing-school teacher since that day, in view of his commissions on the new book, has failed to reach the same conclusion?); and we had obtained the "Manhattan Collection," which was just then a candidate for public favor. Several of the old members of the choir were standing in a group, during an "intermission," expressing their opinions on the merits of the new book, when Deacon Arnold said to the teacher:

"Here is a new tune I should like to have you look at—'Ortonville.' I have hummed it over, and it seems a very good one."

The teacher glanced over it, said they would try it, and very soon the school were singing—

"Majestic sweetness sits enthroned,"

as those words have been sung a thousand times to the sweet and simple notes of—

ORTONVILLE. C. M.   Thomas Hastings, Mus. Doc.

Ma - jes - tic sweet-ness sits enthroned Up - on the Sav - iour's brow: His

head with radiant glory crowned, His lips with grace o'erflow, His lips with grace o'erflow.

Such was my first acquaintance with this piece of sacred music. Little did I then think that it was an acquaintance I was to meet in such different and distant parts of the world, in so many and such varied circumstances, and that was to afford me such peculiar pleasure.

I need hardly say that " Ortonville " became at once a favorite with our school. The new scholars were most apt to strike upon it, if they happened to be in a mood for singing, as they were busy at their winter's tasks—foddering the cattle and other stock at the barn, watering the horses, carrying in the wood for the evening and morning fires in the ample old-fashioned fireplaces, or doing any little chores about the house.

The teacher was pretty sure to select it if the minister or influential members of the congregation came in to see how the school was getting along; as, somehow, they always seemed to be in better time and tune, and do more for the credit of the school, and the satisfaction of those who had raised the subscription, when they sang this, than in singing any other tune. Very soon it was sung everywhere, and those who could sing at all had learned it by rote, at least, as a necessity. The choir were not only better satisfied with themselves, but the minister seemed to preach with more animation, when " Ortonville " was sung upon the Sabbath, and prayer-meetings that were dull and uninteresting would take a new start when "Ortonville" was started. For not only all the new singers could sing, but all the old men and women who had been members of the choir when the country was first settled, and the hardy Puritan pioneers, in the absence of a minister, had what were called "deacon-meetings," the schoolmaster, or whoever was regarded as the best reader in the settlement, reading a sermon.

It was not long before it was found out that we were not alone in our admiration of the new favorite. In the adjoining towns, wherever the singing-schools were using the "Manhattan Collection," they had fallen upon this tune and were singing it just as we were.

Before our singing-school closed I left home to pursue my academic, collegiate, and theological studies, and for a few years following, in connection with my residence at different places, and my travels in different Northern States, I again and again had opportunities of observing that in cities as well as in the country, in centers of intelligence and refinement as well as at my rural home, there was something in "Ortonville" calculated to interest nearly every class of mind, and make it, as soon as it was known in any place, a popular favorite.

With these elements, and our national habit of never sparing our favorites, but pressing them into service for the time, *ad nauseam*, those who heard it once in any place were sure to hear it, to say the least, until they "had heard enough of it," and then it was consigned to comparative neglect.

For a long time I had heard it but rarely; the feeling of dislike at its frequent repetition had worn off, and it again possessed not only its original interest, but was thick clustering with pleasant memories of home, and many of the happiest scenes of my life. I was at length in the interior of a distant Southern State, an invalid, alone, and doubtful of the future. Sabbath came, and with kind, new-found friends, I rode through the pines over a sandy road to a plain, unpainted church, standing in the midst of a piny wood, and bearing the name "Mount Zion." In the rear of this building, comfortably seated and sheltered, a large congregation of slaves was assembled, who were listening to the instructions of an earnest and faithful minister of the gospel. He had just finished reading a hymn as I reached the place, and an old negro slave rose to lead the singing. The lines were given out one by one, and as every voice in that large company seemed to join in the song, never did "Ortonville" sound more sweetly than as it then broke unexpectedly upon my ear. With their rich, melodious voices, and the enthusiasm peculiar to the African, they seemed to pour out all their souls, and, as they sang through the hymn, and those familiar sounds resounded through the grove, the effect upon my feelings can be more easily imagined than described.

During my stay in this neighborhood, a slave died upon one of the plantations, and I was told that I would have an opportunity of witnessing one of their favorite funerals. In those portions of the South where the plantations were largest, and the slaves the most numerous, they were very fond of burying their dead at night, and as near midnight as possible. In case of a funeral, they assembled in large numbers from adjoining plantations, provided with pine-knots, and pieces of fat pine called light-wood, which when ignited made a blaze compared with which our city torch-light processions are most sorry affairs. When all was in readiness, they lighted these torches, formed into a procession, and marched slowly to the distant grave, singing the most solemn music. Sometimes they sang hymns they had committed to memory, but oftener those more tender and plaintive, composed by themselves, that have since been introduced to the people of the North, and of Europe, as plantation melodies. I have never yet seen any statement of the manner in which these melodies, that have moved and melted the hearts of millions on both sides of the Atlantic, were composed. I have been familiar with the secret of their birth and power since my first acquaintance with, and religious labors among, the slaves in 1843. It is preëminently true of these plantation melodies that they were "born, not made." I have been present at the birth of a great many of them—many that

An old-time midnight slave funeral.

I think more tender and pathetic than those that have been given to the world by the various jubilee-singers.

In their religious gatherings the best singer among them was always the leader of the meeting. They usually commenced their services by singing some hymn that they had committed to memory; but the leader always gave out this hymn, one line at a time, in a sing-song tone, much like a chant, and then the audience sang the line he had given out, and so went through the hymn. As the meeting progressed, and their feelings became deeper and deeper, and the excitement rose higher and higher, they at length reached a state of tender or rapturous feeling to which no hymn with which they were familiar gave expression. At this point the leader sang from his heart, or, as musicians say, improvised, both the words and music of a single line. The audience then sang that line with him, as they had sung all the preceding hymns. He then improvised another line, and another, and they sang each one after him, until he had improvised one of those plantation melodies, which, as they gave expression to the glowing hearts of those who first sang them, so, when they have been repeated, they have touched the universal heart. When thus "born," no such words or music were ever forgotten by the leader. It was sung over and over again at succeeding meetings, until some other melody was in like manner improvised, to meet another and perhaps a higher state of religious enthusiasm. In my visits to hundreds of different plantations and congregations, I have heard a great variety of these plantation melodies. Many of them, that were inexpressibly tender and beautiful, were never heard beyond the immediate neighborhood in which they were first sung, and will never be reproduced, unless it be among the songs of the redeemed in heaven.

But to return to this midnight funeral. The appearance of such a procession, winding through the fields and woods, as revealed by their flaming torches, marching slowly to the sound of their wild music, was weird and imposing in the highest degree. This procession was to pass immediately by our door, but, in order to get a fuller view, a small company of us went out a short distance to meet them. We saw them and heard their music in the distance, as they came down a gentle descent, crossed over a small stream, and then marched on some time in silence. As they came near where we stood, we heard their leader announce in the sing-song, chanting style I have already described, the words—

"When I can read my title clear;"

and that long procession, with their flaming fat-pine torches, marched by us with slow and solemn tread, singing that beautiful hymn to the tune of "Ortonville." We followed to the place of burial, listened to their songs and addresses at the grave, and witnessed all the ceremonies to the close. From first to last the scene was impressive beyond description.

A few days after this, as I was taking a lonely horseback-ride to an adjoining parish, I heard the negroes singing in a field that I could not see, lying behind a wood that skirted the road. I stopped my horse for a moment to listen to their music. I could hear no words, but at once distinguished "Ortonville." Soon after I inquired of my host how long these people had been singing this tune, and where they had learned it; and was told that the minister I had seen upon the Sabbath, while on a visit to his relatives in the State of Georgia the fall before, had heard it sung at the meeting of the Synod, and was so much pleased with it that he procured a copy, and in that manner it had been introduced to this place and the places adjacent. At one of those places I was told that they were so much pleased with it that they had sung it over and over one Sabbath-day during the entire intermission.

Time passed on, and in my invalid wanderings I was within the tropics, sailing in the track of Columbus, along the north shore of Hayti. Entering those waters, so often tinged with human blood, that divide this island from the famed Tortugas, as if in harmony with the dark memories that crowded upon the mind, black clouds began to darken the heavens, the thunders rolled, the lightnings gleamed with terrific fury, and amid the most sublime tumult of the elements we were carried along until our little craft dropped anchor in the bay of Port de Paix. The storm and darkness were such that I could not go ashore, and I was that night rocked to sleep on waters where many a pirate-ship, with bloody deck, had ridden securely at anchor, and prepared to set forth again on new missions of pillage and death. This harbor was the chief rendez-vous, the refuge from danger, and retreat from toil, of the buccaneers that for years infested these seas, and whose piratical plunderings for so long a time made their names a terror to all within their reach. How-ever, not being particularly superstitious, I slept sound-ly for the night.

In the morning I left our little vessel and received —what is ever so grateful to a wanderer on a foreign shore, and especially to one who has any sympathy with the command, "Go teach all nations"—a welcome to the residence of a countryman, to a missionary's humble home. Ay, noble men and women are they, who, forgetful of themselves, and alone for the honor of the Master that they serve, leaving the comforts and amenities of a Christian civilization, toil on through life amid manifold discouragements, endeavoring to in-struct and elevate the degraded, and, above all else, anxious to

"Allure to brighter worlds and lead the way."

And yet, like those whose own minds are so degraded and debauched that they can not conceive of purity and virtue in any character, there are those who are so utterly ignorant and unconscious of the lofty sentiments that animate these self-sacrificing missionaries, that they are ever finding, in base, unworthy, and ignoble objects, the grand motive of their life-work. Such may well ponder the life of unparalleled Christian heroism of the great Apostle to the Gentiles, of which the undoubted and sufficient motive was a constraining LOVE!

Evening darkened around the dwelling of the missionary, and a little group of natives assembled for religious worship. I sat in that little room and listened to the words of instruction, praise, and prayer, with indescribably strange emotions, for all was in a language that I did not understand. As the services proceeded, a hymn was read by the missionary with peculiar interest and emotion, and the dark group sang in the familiar strains of "Ortonville":

> " Beni soit bien qui chaque jour
> Nous comble de ses biens,
> Et dont s'inconvenable amour
> A romptu nos liens."

What a change—what a change! The haunts of bloody pirates giving place to the home of the missionary of the cross; the wild, agonized shrieks of their murdered victims succeeded by the sweet and peaceful notes of "Ortonville!" And so this tune has often been sung where sounds of direst woe and wretchedness had long been heard, and so it doubtless will be, and onward to the millennium.

As I once returned from a small church on the banks of the Savannah River, where it had been sung, the friend whose hospitality I was enjoying remarked:

"My brother-in-law, a missionary, told me he first heard that tune, and since had often sung it, on Mount Zion, in Jerusalem, and it sounded most sweetly there."

And thus it has been sung in many a land and clime by that heroic missionary band which now encircles the globe with celestial light.

But this narrative would swell to a volume were I to relate in detail all the sweet, sacred, and delightful memories associated with "Ortonville." In all my long invalid wanderings, and in all the years in which I have been permitted to labor actively in the Master's service, both "in the Brush" and elsewhere, it has often been my happy lot to recognize and greet in the most varied and striking circumstances the favorite I first learned to love in that country singing-school. Its gentle, soothing notes have broken sweetly upon my ear in crowded city churches; in quiet meetings for prayer; in large, unpainted, barn-like edifices erected for Christian sanctuaries; in rude log churches crowded with devout worshipers; in basket-meetings, camp-meetings, and in all varieties of gatherings for the worship of Almighty God. Often, very often, it has inspired my devotions as I have mingled, for the first time, with households gathered for family worship. With adoring recognition of the Fatherhood of God, and with loving recognition of the brotherhood of man, it has been my happy, happy lot thus to worship with uncounted hundreds of families —among them the most cultivated and refined, and the most ignorant, neglected, and lowly of God's poor. In very long horseback-journeys, for days, weeks, and months together, as I have ridden over bleak, desolate "barrens," through dense, dark forests, along deep, narrow ravines and valleys, and up and over rough and rugged mountains, nearly every night has found me under a different roof, enjoying the rough or refined hospitality of a new-found family. As they have invited me to "take the books" (the Bible and hymn-book) and lead the devotions of the family, often in the most remote and lowly cabins, I have been surprised and delighted, as I was in the tropics, with the familiar notes of "Ortonville."

As I write these lines my memory is far more busy than my pen. I think of my wanderings in many different States, and of the cabins in which I have briefly rehearsed the old, old story, and by kind words of entreaty, and in reverent words of prayer, attempted to "allure to brighter worlds, and lead the way." I have knelt in prayer in many a home along the banks of the

Rappahannock, the James, the Cape Fear, the Santee, the Savannah, the Tennessee, the Cumberland, the Ohio, the Mississippi, the Missouri, the San Joaquin, the Sacramento, and many other rivers. So I have knelt and prayed in homes along the shores of the stormy Atlantic and the peaceful Pacific. Very often the inmates, at first startled, and then delighted, by the strangeness of my visit, have told me that my voice was the first ever lifted in prayer beneath their roofs. Though in multitudes of such homes no member of the family had ever learned a single letter of the alphabet of their mother-tongue, and all were barefooted, and more destitute and ignorant than the most of my readers will be able to conceive, they have received me in their homes with a hospitality so hearty and cordial, and have thanked me, and bidden me come again, with such warm words and such abounding tears, that my own have welled and flowed responsive to theirs; and as I have spoken my farewell words, so often final, and ridden away with new impressions of the power of the Saviour's name and love to touch and melt the rudest minds, my happy heart has found full expression in the tender notes and sweet words of my favorite tune and hymn :

> " Majestic sweetness sits enthroned
> Upon the Saviour's brow ;
> His head with radiant glories crowned,
> His lips with grace o'erflow.

" No mortal can with him compare,
　Among the sons of men;
Fairer is he than all the fair
　Who fill the heavenly train.

" He saw me plunged in deep distress,
　And flew to my relief;
For me he bore the shameful cross,
　And carried all my grief.

" Since from his bounty I receive
　Such proofs of love divine,
Had I a thousand hearts to give,
　Lord, they should all be thine."

NOTE.—Returning from one of my visits to Hayti, more than twenty-five years ago, I communicated to Professor Hastings, at his old home in Amity Street, New York, several of the facts related in this chapter. He then gave me the history of the tune as follows:

" I was anxious to write just as simple a tune as possible, to be sung by children. I sat at my instrument, and played, until this tune was completely formed in my mind.

" Not long after, a boy came from the printer with a note, saying he needed another tune to fill out a page or form. I sat down at my instrument, played it again, thought it would do, wrote it out, and sent it to the office, little dreaming that I should hear from it, as I have, from almost every part of the world."

CHAPTER XVI.

I do not propose to give anything like a full account or even a summary of the work accomplished in my special mission by all these long rides and years of earnest and cheerful labor in the Brush. That has not been my object. It has been rather to describe the manner of performing these labors, the incidents connected with them, and to portray the character, manners, customs, and peculiarities of the people who received me so cordially, and with whom I mingled so freely in their rude homes. But I should fail to give a full and true idea of their social and moral condition, especially as indicated by their want of education, and their destitution of Bibles, if I did not give some of the results of these labors. I have described the manner in which I explored different counties, organized or reorganized Bible societies, and secured the appointment of distributors to canvass them.

One of these men, Mr. Guier, a well-known citizen

of the county, visited five hundred and fifty-eight families, of whom one hundred and sixty—more than one fourth—were destitute of the Bible. They contained four hundred and thirty-five persons. In sixty-four of them either the husband or wife, or both (according to their own statements), were members of some Protestant church. Sixty-two Bibles and ninety Testaments were sold, amounting to one hundred and fourteen dollars and eighty-five cents; and thirty-three Bibles and six Testaments were given away, amounting to ten dollars and forty cents. Mr. Guier communicated to me the following facts in connection with his labors:

"I visited a man at his house, and asked him if he had a Bible. He said no. I told him he ought to have one. He said he was not able to buy. I told him that I could sell so cheap that any man could buy. He said he had not paid for his land yet, and he had no time to read. I then took up my saddle-bags to go, and offered him a Bible as a gift. He said: 'Stop, sir; I will pay you for it. I would not have my neighbor to know that you gave me a Bible.'

"I found a poor widow at work in her garden, who told me she had no Bible, and no money to buy one with. She was a church-member, and very anxious to have a Bible, but she was not willing to receive one as a gift. She said she had a kind neighbor, who would always lend her money when he had it; but her little son was some distance from home, at a blacksmith-shop, and she could not send for the money. As she was so anxious to get a Bible, I found her son, and went with him to see the neighbor, who loaned her one dollar and twenty-five cents to get the Bible she wanted. May God bless it to her!

"I was one day taken so sick that I had to stop by the side of the road a half-hour or more. I then rode on to a cabin, and told the lady I was very unwell, and asked if she could let me have a bed to lie upon. She seemed alarmed, and said she would have no objection if her husband was at home. I told her I was very ill and could not ride, and that I was distributing Bibles. She at once told me to get down and come in, and she nursed me with the greatest care and attention until her husband came. On his arrival I explained to him why I was there; and he said they would take the best care of me they could, which they did until the next morning. They told me they had no Bible and no money. I offered to pay them for keeping me, but they would receive no pay. I then gave them a Bible, which they received very thankfully. The lady was a church-member, and I have heard that her husband has since been converted and united with the church.

"I asked a man in a field if he had a Bible. He said he did not know, but his wife could tell. I went to the house, and she told me they had no Bible, but she was very anxious to get one. Her husband came in, and I told him his wife had no Bible, and he ought to get her one. He said he would like to have a Bible, as the leaves would make good wadding for his gun; and made a good many other remarks of the same nature in regard to the Bible. His wife sat and wept all the time, and, as I thought it useless to talk with him longer, I prepared to leave, and she handed me the Bible she had been looking at. I told her to keep it. She said she could not—she had no money. I told her that made no difference; the Bible Society would give it to her. She was greatly rejoiced at receiving the unexpected gift.

"I found an old sailor who was plowing for a neighbor to get corn for his family, who told me he had no Bible. He had been a member of the church about two years, and seemed to be very religious. He was very glad to see my Bibles, but said he could not buy one. He had no money, lived on rented land, and could with difficulty support his family. I told him that, if he was too poor to buy, he was not too poor to read, and that the Bible Society enabled me to give him a Bible. He received it with astonishment and joy, and praised God aloud that he had lived to see the day when the poor were supplied with the Bible without money and without price. I left him in the field, shouting aloud his praises to God that he now had the blessed Bible to read.

"I saw a man about sixty years old, who had raised a large family and was now living with his third wife, standing by his field and looking at a lot of fine colts. I asked him if he had a Bible. He said, No; he had no use for a Bible. I then asked him if he had ever had a Bible in his family. He said, No; he had no use for a Bible. After doing my best to sell him a Bible, I told him the Bible Society made it my duty to offer him one as a gift. But he refused to receive it. I was told by one of his neighbors that he did not think he had been at church for years.

"The country I have visited is exceedingly rough and broken. It has been very hard work to climb all the hills and knobs, and hunt up all the people scattered over them, and up and down the valleys. But I have endeavored to explore it faithfully, and leave no family unvisited, and without the offer of a Bible. I have been in a good many families and neighborhoods that had never before been visited by a Bible distributor. I was born in this county, and when solicited to undertake this work I thought it was entirely unnecessary. I had no idea that twenty families could be found in the county without a Bible. And now, before the work is half completed, the exploration reveals such facts as these."

In the thorough exploration and supply of another county, Father J. G. Kasey, the venerable Bible distributor, visited six hundred and fifty-five families, of whom one hundred and twenty-seven—nearly one fifth —were destitute of the Bible. Eight of the families supplied were entirely without education; and six families refused to receive the Bible as a gift. He sold in the county one hundred and forty-one Bibles and Testaments, amounting to sixty-three dollars and ninety-one cents; and gave away eighty-one Bibles and Testaments, amounting to twenty dollars and seventy-five cents. Father Kasey's labors were eminently of a missionary character. He sat down with the people at their firesides, exhorted Christians to greater fidelity and zeal in their Master's service, kindly warned and urged sinners to flee to Christ for salvation, and then, bowing with them in prayer, humbly and earnestly besought God's blessing upon them. What enterprise is more Christian, or what work more blessed, than the distribution of the Word of God, accompanied with such labors? He said:

"I have cause to rejoice for the success I have met with in supplying the people with the Holy Bible, and imparting religious instruction. I have been able to have religious conversation and prayer with almost every family I have visited, and from all I could learn I was induced to believe that it made a good impression on the most of them. I found a comfortable

home one night with a kind old brother, of the Episcopal Church. After supper we sat in the parlor, and
he went on to speak of his efforts to train up his children in the fear of the Lord; but none of them were
yet Christians. He had become discouraged, and seemed
almost to give them up. I advised him to continue
his prayer and efforts, believing that God would bring
them in—if not in his day, when he was gone. Some
of his children were present, and my conversation and
prayer seemed to make a good impression upon the
family. Some time afterward several of his children
were converted and united with the church.

"In my travels I called at a house where they had
no Bible or Testament, but gladly received one as a
gift. After conversation and prayer, I exhorted the
woman to seek the Lord. She wept very bitterly as
I addressed her, and said she intended to do so. She
was as deeply affected as any person I ever saw, and
as I bade her good-by she held me by the hand several minutes, refusing to let me go. She said she had
not been in the habit of attending church, but she
would do so from that time. I pointed her to the
Lamb of God, and she promised to seek religion with
all her heart. She said I must attend a meeting that
had been appointed to be held in the neighborhood.
I did so, and found her happy in the love of God, and
she has since united with the Church of Christ. I
afterward saw her husband, who was a very wicked

man. He seemed deeply affected, and promised to seek religion; and I trust he, too, may be converted.

"I called upon another family, where the man had previously had a Bible, but had burned it. Afterward he became convicted, and was anxious for another. I sold him a Bible, exhorted him to become a Christian, and trust he will be a better man.

"I found another man who had lived to a good old age, and had twenty children now living, three having gone to the eternal world. The family was destitute of any portion of the Bible. I gave him the Word of God, exhorted him to seek the Lord, prayed with him, hoping that the good Lord would save him and his large family, as they were all irreligious. He received my visit thankfully.

"I rode up to a very poor cabin, in a hollow, and found a woman plowing with one horse. Several little children, very ragged, were playing near her. I asked her if she had a Bible. She said she had not—she was very poor; her husband was dead, and she had several children, none of whom were large enough to help her, and she was trying to raise something for them to eat. I asked her if she did not want a Bible. She said, 'Oh, yes, very much, but I am too poor to buy one.' I told her it was my business to seek out the poor and the destitute, and supply them with the Bible. I then gave her one, which she received with a great deal of thankfulness. I told her the Lord had

promised to be a God to the widow and the fatherless,
and exhorted her to put her trust in him. As I rode
away, she followed me with her thanks, and her prayers
that the Lord would bless me.

"There were many other interesting circumstances,
that made a lasting impression upon my mind. The
good accomplished by the Lord, through his humble
servant, by this distribution of the Word of God, will
not be known in this world. My heart is in this work,
for I know I am engaged in a good work."

Mr. Lutes was commissioned to undertake the re-
exploration and supply of a county where I had reorganized a society that had been inactive for many
years. During the first three months of his labor he
visited six hundred and thirty-three families, of whom
one hundred and twenty-eight—more than one fifth—
were destitute of the Bible. He sold two hundred
and twenty-eight Bibles and Testaments, amounting to
one hundred and seventeen dollars and six cents, and
gave away forty-five, amounting to ten dollars and forty-nine cents. In speaking of his great amazement
at finding so many families destitute of the Bible, he
said:

"Experience has taught me that a poor and very
incorrect estimate will be made in regard to this matter
while we remain at home—while we look upon our
Bibles and say: ' How cheap such books are ! Surely
everybody must have them.' I have found, to my

I gave her a Bible, and as I rode away she followed me with
her thanks and her prayers.

great surprise, fifteen families in which either the husband or wife, or both, were members of some Protestant church, and had no Bible. I visited three destitute families in succession: the first, a poor widow; the second, husband and wife, both members of the church; the third wanted *spiritual-rapping books*, but was finally persuaded to buy a Bible. I gave a poor man a Bible, and next Sabbath he and his wife were both at church, a very uncommon sight. I visited a school-teacher, a liberally educated Irishman, but very poor. He said he had neither Bible nor Testament, and that he should like a large Testament in his family. He cheerfully paid me for one. I visited a poor widow, a church-member, who had been a housekeeper many years, had children married and removed to a distant State; but she had no Bible. Poor creature! I gave her one, and she wished me to fill out the family record for her; but she had neglected the matter so long that she had lost all trace of the date of births, marriages, and deaths. In the next family the husband seemed indifferent about the book, but the wife wanted it, which I readily discovered. ' I'm poor,' said he; and his wife said, 'He was unable to work during the summer.' ' I have Bibles for thirty cents.' 'Well, I haven't money enough to pay for one.' 'You can have it at your own price.' 'I don't like to take a book that way.' 'It makes no difference; I am authorized to make this offer to you: you can have it

for ten or fifteen cents.' 'Certainly; I'd give ten cents
for a Bible any time.' This saved his pride. He has
been greatly pleased with his Bible, and whenever I
pass his house he comes out and asks me questions
relative to my success, and gives me directions how to
pass over the country, as if he were one of the 'Ex-
ecutive Committee.' I sold a Bible to an Irish toll-
gate - keeper. I had been on the pike about a mile,
and asked him the toll. 'Nothing, sir; are you a doctor?' 'No, sir, I am a bookseller. Do you wish to
buy?' 'I reckon not; I work six days on the road,
and on Sundays I read a newspaper.' 'Have you a
Bible?' 'No, sir.' 'Wouldn't you like to have one?'
'I believe I would, but I have no money.' 'It makes
no difference; if you have no Bible and want one,
I'll leave it.' 'I don't like to take it in that way.'
'No difference; if you'll read it carefully, we shall be
well paid.' 'Why,' said he, when I told him the
price was twenty-five cents, ' in Ireland the bind-
ing would be more than that; and I'll pay you the
first time you pass this gate.' I went down a creek
nearly a mile to see a family, and came back. When
some three hundred yards from the toll-gate, I saw
the keeper sitting upon the ground, leaning against
the house, perfectly absorbed in reading his Bible. He
has since paid me for it, and he and his wife are
greatly pleased with it. Staid all night with a poor
family; wife a church-member, and no Bible; husband

careless, but wife anxious to have one. In the morning I took a thirty-cent Bible from my saddle-bags and commenced filling out the family record. Said he: 'I don't want you to give me that book. I don't charge you for staying all night.' 'I find you destitute, and wish you to have a Bible.' He stood for some time, then went to a drawer, and, finding a quarter, gave it to me, saying it was all he had, and kindly invited me to call again.

"One day I visited twenty-one families, eleven of whom were destitute of the Bible. Another day I visited twenty families, and found ten destitute of the Bible. During the spring I left a box of books at the house of a magistrate, as a depositary, while I visited the neighborhood. Said he, 'Do you think you will find anybody here without a Bible?' 'I don't know, sir.' 'Some two years since,' said he, 'I looked around and could not find but one man destitute, and him I supplied.'

"I commenced my labors, and found his partner in a mill destitute; then one of his hands, having a family; then an old neighbor, who was a church-member. The squire gave it up, and said it was *necessary* to have colporteurs.

"In some of these destitute neighborhoods they told me that no person had ever visited them before with Bibles and Testaments. They occupied a very broken country; their houses were cabins scattered over the hills and up narrow valleys, with very small patches of ground fenced in around them, generally with no bars, and always with no gates. I traveled among them, following the rocky beds of the streams, and frequently led my horse up and down the steep hills, and pulled down fences, till at night I was so tired I could scarcely walk. I have had many discouragements, many taunts and sneers to bear from those who had not the love of God shed abroad in their hearts; but then I have had the smiles, the assistance, and the warm coöperation of Christians to hold up my feeble hands, and cheer up my desponding heart. I have found such families with six, eight, and ten Bibles in a single house; I have found many who have thrown open their doors and bid me welcome to the hospitality of their homes, who, by their kind words and their questions respecting my work, caused me to forget the sneers and taunts of others, and made me adore the Almighty for the success with which he crowned the labors of his servants employed in his vineyard. May the Lord inspire the minds of Christians with greater zeal for the dissemination of his Word!"

In another county Mr. Temple visited seven hundred and three families, of whom eighty-three were destitute of the Bible. His sales of Bibles and Testaments amounted to ninety dollars and forty cents, and his donations to the destitute to forty-three dollars and twenty-five cents. The exploration of the county revealed a much greater amount of poverty and destitution of the Word of God than he had expected to find. The following are some of the incidents connected with his labors:

"A poor widow with five children had no Bible, but she had a small Testament, which she got her children to read to her, as it was difficult for her to read such small print. She had long been anxious to get a Bible, and was delighted when I told her I had Bibles for sale, but she feared she had not money enough to get one. She was greatly pleased with the large Testament and Psalms, as she could read the print. She gathered together all the money she and her children had, and made up twenty-five cents, for which I gave her the Testament and Psalms. In another neighborhood I was told by a good many persons of a poor widow that had no Bible, who was very anxious to get one. Her Bible had been wet and ruined in moving from North Carolina, and she had been several years without one. She had been saving money from the sale of eggs and chickens to get enough to buy a Bible. When I reached the place, I found a poor cabin in an old field, and everything indicating great poverty. A chair was standing in the door, which was open, but there was no one at home. I wrote in a Bible, 'Presented by the Bible Society,' and left it in the chair, and rode on.

"I heard of one old man who had nine grown

children, and had never had a Bible or Testament in his family. I was told that he was a skeptic and very profane, and that I had better not visit him, as he would treat me roughly. I found him plowing, and talked with him a long time about farming, and at length about our dependence upon God for crops, and finally told him I was selling Bibles. He invited me to dine with him, and I went to his house and sold him a family Bible, and also sold Bibles to a married son and daughter. The old man did not use a profane word during my visit, and I was never treated better by any man. He thanked me for my visit, and begged me to call on him whenever I passed that way.

"I visited a house and found no one at home. As the family was evidently very poor, and I had learned that they had no Bible, I wrote on one, 'Presented by the Bible Society,' and left it between the logs, near the door, where they would be sure to find it when they came home. I rode on about two miles, and called at another house. As soon as I showed my Bibles, one of the women said she was sorry she was not at home, as she had no Bible and had long been anxious to get one. She thought she had money enough to get a thirty-cent Bible, and if I would go back with her she would buy one if she could. I then told her I had left a Bible for her, and where she would find it, and she thanked me very warmly for the gift.

"I visited another family that had no Bible, and sold them one. As the children were looking at my books, I heard a little girl, about ten years old, say that she wished she had money enough to buy one of these Bibles; that her mother, when she talked with her before she died, had told her she must get a Bible as soon as she could, and read it, and be a good girl, and meet her in heaven. I inquired her history, and learned that she was an orphan. I then gave her a Bible, and she commenced reading it. Dinner was soon ready, but she could not be induced to stop reading long enough to eat, and when I left the house she was still reading her new Bible."

Father Eggen, a veteran Bible distributor, said: "One man told me he had a neighbor who was very poor, who had no Bible, and I gave him one to send to him. I afterward called on this family, not knowing it was the same. The house was without floor or loft, and was inclosed by nailing rough boards upon posts that were driven into the ground. It had a stick-and-mud chimney on the outside, and was without floor of any kind, the family living on the ground. The man followed making split-bottomed chairs, and was very poor indeed, but he insisted upon paying for the Bible that had been sent to him, and did so.

"In one neighborhood where there was a small supply of Bibles and Testaments at a store, the man who had them, a professing Christian, insisted that

14

there was no necessity for employing a distributor to go around; said that, if people wanted Bibles, they could easily come to the store and get them. I, however, went through this neighborhood, and found in one day fifteen families without a Bible. Some of them were very large families, and had been destitute for many years."

It is now (August 1, 1881) more than twenty-three years since I resigned my commission as an agent of the American Bible Society. During the last week I have visited the Bible House, examined their well-preserved files of letters, and read the correspondence between Secretary McNeill and myself during the last months of my connection with the Society. Some extracts from these letters will appropriately close this brief review of "work accomplished in the Southwest."

LOUISVILLE, KENTUCKY, April 2, 1858.

Rev. JAMES H. McNEILL, *Secretary of the American Bible Society, New York.*

MY DEAR BROTHER: Herewith you have my annual report. . . . My duties the last year, as well as all the other years of my agency, have involved a great deal of labor and self-denial. The field assigned to my supervision is very large, and, in order to accomplish thoroughly the great work of "home supply," it has been necessary for me to visit every county on horseback. I have thus ridden many thousands of miles, exposed to all the extremes of heat and cold, traveling over the roughest of roads, fording rivers, penetrating the wildest regions, eating the coarsest food, and sleeping in the worst of beds. But I have everywhere received a cordial welcome, and I wish here to record my testimony that such service in such a cause is a blessed service. I weep tears of gratitude that God has permitted me thus to labor for the dissemination of his Word. And now that his Spirit is being poured out so copiously all over our land,* I rejoice exceedingly that I have been permitted to coöperate with others in sowing so much "good seed" against these times of refreshing from on high. I pray that all the seed thus sown may bear abundant fruit.

Yours cordially,
II. W. PIERSON.

LOUISVILLE, KENTUCKY, *May* 28, 1858.

Rev. JAMES H. MCNEILL, *Secretary of the American Bible Society.*

MY DEAR BROTHER: I reached the city on my return from the western part of the State on Wednesday morning, after an absence of more than six weeks. The tour was one of the most successful and gratifying I have ever made. I find here letters and papers that have been accumulating during my absence, and have been exceedingly busy in posting myself up, and getting square with the world. All your anniversary excitements have come off while I was in the Brush, and I have been trying to find out where you have left the world. I have read the "Christian Intelligencer's" full report of the meeting of the American Tract Society. I should have been delighted to be an eye-witness of the fight. † On my last tour I learned that, of nine hundred and twenty-five families visited in G—— County, one hundred and sixty had *no part* of the Word of God in their houses—not a leaf or a letter! Oh, it is a burning shame to American Christianity, and especially to the American Bible Society, that such facts as these can be reported in the forty-third year of its history! But I am speaking warmly, nevertheless truly.

I leave the city to-day, and expect to spend the Sabbath at Paducah, Kentucky, and go on to Princeton early in the week. I have been unanimously elected President and Professor of Mental and Moral Philosophy in Cumberland College, at Princeton, Kentucky, and the terms are so very liberal, and the people are so very earnest to have me accept the appointment, that I am going down

---

* The great revival that followed the financial revulsion of 1857.

† On the slavery question.

to see them and give them my answer. The probabilities are, that I shall accept, and send you my resignation, to take effect as soon as I can close up the work in several counties where it is nearly completed. I will thank you not to make this matter public until I resign formally. I write now in order to have you take steps in regard to my successor. I feel a good deal of solicitude to have one appointed who will carry on the work as I have been prosecuting it. I think there will be a general solicitude on the subject over the field. I have, therefore, kept this college matter a secret here, in order than you might have more time for considering the subject before my resignation is known to the public. I will cheerfully render any advice or aid in my power in the matter.

Yours *ut semper*, H. W. PIERSON,
Agent of the American Bible Society.

BIBLE HOUSE, ASTOR PLACE, NEW YORK, *June* 28, 1858.

REV. H. W. PIERSON.

MY DEAR BROTHER: . . . But what shall I say of the announcement of your purpose to leave this good work? Only that I regret it most deeply. I stated to the Agency Committee your intention and its reasons. Of course, they could not oppose your wishes, and directed me to inquire for your successor. I am anxious to find a man who will carry on the work as you have been doing. Can you name any one? Do so if you know the man. But I trust you have ere this reconsidered the matter, and will withhold your resignation. In my opinion, your present position is one of far more usefulness than the presidency of Cumberland College, if that were the greatest college in the land. Let me hear from you soon.

Cordially yours, JAMES H. McNEILL,
Corresponding Secretary of the American Bible Society.

LOUISVILLE, KENTUCKY, *July* 9, 1858.

Rev. JAMES H. McNEILL, *Secretary of the American Bible Society,*
 New York.

MY DEAR BROTHER: Since my last report I have completed my annual exploration of the seven counties lying west of the Tennessee River, and known as "Jackson's Purchase"—from the fact that General Jackson was the agent of the United States Government in buying it from the Indians. I have been greatly delighted at what I have learned, in all these counties, of the progress that has been made in the good work of Bible distribution during the past year. A little more than a year ago I organized the Paducah and Vicinity Bible Society, including McCracken, Marshall, Calloway, and Graves Counties. I immediately visited and preached in all those counties, secured colporteurs sent them Bibles, and made full arrangements to have them thoroughly explored and supplied. I have already ordered more than fifteen hundred dollars' worth of books for this Society, and the good work has progressed most encouragingly. One of the distributors reports: "I have been laboring in one part of the most destitute portion of the county. The part of which I speak is a slope in the northeast corner of the county, embracing, perhaps, a hundred families. In this whole slope there can scarcely be said to be any church. Most of the people are uneducated, there having been no schools. I one day visited seventeen families, nine of whom had no Bible, and several of whom had no book of any kind in their houses."

It is impossible to give to any one who has not a personal knowledge of the country thus visited any adequate conception of the good accomplished by these labors. Less than half the county has been explored, but I have made arrangements with Father Gregory, the distributor, to continue the work until every family has been visited and all the destitute supplied.

After completing my work in these counties I went to Columbus, Kentucky. Here I found a very noble work had been accomplished. I have ordered for them during the year more than seven hundred dollars' worth of Bibles. I next visited Hickman, Fulton County. The society that I organized there last year has not been able to secure a colporteur, but hope soon to make arrangements to have their county supplied. I have already ordered about twenty-five hundred dollars' worth of Bibles for the "Purchase," and more than one thousand dollars' worth more will be needed to complete the work that is in such successful progress. The friends of the cause in all these counties are astonished and delighted at what has been accomplished already, and the bright prospects for the future. *Laus Deo.* Your brother in Christ, H. W. PIERSON,
Agent of the American Bible Society.

Rev. H. W. PIERSON.

MY DEAR BROTHER: I have just received yours of the 9th instant, giving an account of your visit to the seven counties lying west of the Tennessee River, and known as "Jackson's Purchase," where you have the satisfaction of observing decided and gratifying progress in the good work of Bible distribution during the past year. In reading your report of what has been accomplished, I was almost as much "delighted" as you could have been in seeing with your own eyes the progress of the good work.

And, now, can you reconcile it to your own heart and conscience to abandon such a field and such a work? I confess I do not see how you can, and I hope to receive very soon your ultimate decision declining the call to the college at Princeton. Did you receive my last at Louisville? Since writing it I have had a letter from our friend Rev. W. F. Talbot, of Columbus, Kentucky, *protesting against your being allowed to leave the Bible work*, and urging us to do all in our power to retain you. I answered him that I hoped you would not be tempted to leave us by any considerations other than those of clear and imperative duty; and, as your own mind had not been fully made up when you last wrote, I thought it most likely that you would continue in the Agency.

Now, let me again, in behalf of our committee, in behalf of the great work now in progress in that field, and in behalf of the future interests of the Bible cause there, protest against your desertion! Think of the *many friends* whom you have gained for yourself personally, while you were securing their affections and coöperation for the Bible Society, who will be in great danger of falling back into their former indifference and inactivity, should they lose your active support. In fact, I do not see how we can let you go! If you do go, it will be in the face of our remonstrances, and those of every friend of the cause in your field. Please let us hear from you at your earliest convenience.

Cordially yours,

JAMES H. McNEILL,
Corresponding Secretary of the American Bible Society.

Notwithstanding the earnestness of these entreaties, I felt compelled to retire from this work. No one could appreciate its importance more highly than, from my personal knowledge of its needs, I did. But for more than ten years since my graduation from the theological seminary, I had been constantly " on the wing." As stated in my opening chapter, I had spent five years as an invalid wanderer. I had roamed over the Southern States nearly a year, had made two visits to the Island of Hayti, and spent a second winter in the South. I had then entered upon these itinerant labors, in which I had spent nearly five years more. I was not weary of the work, but I wanted change; I sighed for rest and an opportunity to study—to commune again with my beloved books that had remained unopened during all these years. In addition to these personal desires, my labors had revealed the imperative demand for the liberal education of as many as possible of the young men in the wide region I had so thoroughly explored; and a large number of my "many friends" had signified to me their strong desire to place their sons in the college should I accept the appointment. I therefore wrote my resignation, as follows:

LOUISVILLE, KENTUCKY, *July* 12, 1858.

Rev. JAMES H. McNEILL, *Secretary of the American Bible Society, New York.*

MY DEAR BROTHER: I have already informed you that I had been elected President and Professor of Mental and Moral Philosophy in Cumberland College, Princeton, Kentucky.

After mature and prayerful consideration of the whole subject, I have decided to accept the appointment; and I therefore resign my commission as Agent of the American Bible Society for Western Kentucky.

It is not without deep emotion that I thus sunder my official connection with this noble institution. For nearly five years I have labored to promote its interests, and during this entire period all my correspondence and intercourse with its different officers has been of the most pleasant character. I can not recall a single word or act that has marred the harmony of our relations.

The field assigned me is very large—with meager facilities for traveling—and on this account my duties have been very laborious. I have again and again *ridden on horseback* over all the counties southward from this city to the Tennessee line, and westward to the Mississippi River. I have preached repeatedly in all of them, solicited donations, secured colporteurs, ordered Bibles for them, and made full arrangements to have all the families visited, and every destitute household supplied with the inestimable WORD by sale or gift. I have thus ridden thousands of miles over the roughest roads, exposed to every variety of weather.

But, though laborious and self-denying, I have found this a blessed service—rich in *physical* as well as spiritual rewards. Commencing with lungs diseased, and a body enfeebled by years of ill health, I have rejoiced in an almost constant sense of returning strength and vigor, up to the present moment—until now there are few that can endure more physical toil than I can.

My numerous reports have furnished abundant yet very inadequate evidences of the rich spiritual rewards that have crowned these efforts to scatter the "good seed" of the Word. Again and again the sower and the reaper have rejoiced together. Hundreds and thousands of families, that were living without the sacred volume, are now rejoicing in its blessed light; and other multitudes that are still destitute will soon receive the heavenly boon. And God's blessing will surely attend his own Word. "For as the snow cometh down, and the rain from heaven," etc., etc.

Be assured, my dear brother, I shall ever cherish a profound and lively interest in the operations of the American Bible Society. Though Providence seems to call me to another sphere of duty, I shall ever rejoice to do all in my power to promote its interests. I shall ever cherish the most pleasant recollections of my connection with it, and especially of my correspondence and associations with you.

Praying that God may richly bless you, and all its officers, agents, and friends, I remain

Yours in the best of bonds,

H. W. PIERSON.

In the following October I mounted my horse at Princeton, Kentucky, and rode to Hopkinsville to attend the Louisville Annual Conference, as I had regularly done so many years before. In a copy of the "Hopkinsville Mercury," October 20, 1858, now before me, I find the following notice of my address, and the action of the Conference upon that occasion:

The Rev. H. W. Pierson, of the Presbyterian Church, having labored for a number of years, with eminent success in this State, as an agent of the American Bible Society, appeared in Conference on Tuesday morning and announced that he had resigned the office in the discharge of which he had made the acquaintance of nearly all the Methodist ministers in Kentucky, as well as those of other churches. His remarks, in which he expressed the deep regret and pain with which he took this step, were very appropriate, simple, and touching, and were responded to in very handsome terms by Bishop Kavenaugh, and other members of the Conference. The following resolution was then unanimously adopted:

Resolved, That we express our high appreciation of the faithfulness and efficiency of Rev. H. W. Pierson, A. M., as agent of the American Bible Society in Western Kentucky; that we most cordially reciprocate the feelings of brotherly love which he has this day expressed, and that we fervently pray the blessings of the great Head of the Church upon him, wherever his lot, in the providence of God, may be cast.

A. BROWN,
THOMAS BOTTOMLY,
R. DEARING.

CUMBERLAND COLLEGE, PRINCETON, KENTUCKY, *October* 12, 1858.

Rev. JAMES II. McNEILL, *Secretary of the American Bible Society,*
     New York.

MY DEAR BROTHER: . . . I have had a very pleasant time at
Conference. The "Bible Committee" presented a most flattering
resolution in regard to my agency labors. I made the Conference a
valedictory address, and the Bishop and others responded to it in
the kindest manner. Another resolution, commending my labors,
etc., was then offered, and the members were requested to vote upon
it by rising, when the whole Conference arose to their feet. I could
but be deeply moved by their expressions of kindness, and many
tears were shed by them. I confess I am amazed and astounded at
the kind words I have received on every hand. I had no idea that
my labors had made such an impression upon the public mind. To
God be all the praise!

Yours, as ever,

II. W. PIERSON.

CONCLUSION OF BIBLE WORK.

To see what I have seen, and to know what I
have known, of the good accomplished by my labors,
have been abundant compensation for all my travels
and for all my toils; and I await, with bright and
happy anticipations, the fuller revelations and rewards
of a blissful eternity.

LABORS FOR THE COLLEGE.

I entered upon my duties as President of Cumberland College, at Princeton, Kentucky, the second Monday in September, 1858. Of the commencement of
my labors there I wrote as follows:

CUMBERLAND COLLEGE, PRINCETON, KENTUCKY, *October* 12, 1858.
Rev. JAMES H. McNEILL, *Secretary of the American Bible Society,
New York.*

MY DEAR BROTHER: I have been very anxious to write you ever
since I reached here, but have been so very busy that I could not
get the time. I have had a great deal to do here in the commencement of my duties, and then I have been absent every Sabbath, and
a portion of each week, attending presbyteries, synods, etc., to promote the interests of the college. Its friends are very sanguine in
regard to its prospects. They think they have not been as good for
many years. All the religious bodies that I have visited, the newspapers, and the public at large, seem interested in my success, and
are doing all that they can for the college. I hope that I may do a
great deal of good in this work.

Yours as ever,
H. W. PIERSON.

My labors here until 1861 were not less exhausting
than they had been since I entered upon my Bible work
in 1853. In addition to my duties in the college, I
traveled extensively, "electioneering" for students, as
was the custom in that region. Their numbers increased
to such an extent that we needed an additional building.
I appealed to the people of the village and the county,
and they responded most nobly by subscribing twenty
thousand dollars, and erecting a college edifice, with a
large assembly hall, library, recitation and all other
needed rooms. I had the pleasure of taking my esteemed friend, the Right Rev. B. B. Smith, D. D.,
Bishop of the Protestant Episcopal Church in Kentucky,
through the building, on one of his annual parochial
visits to the village, and he pronounced it the most

perfect and beautiful specimen of architecture in the State.

The attack on Fort Sumter, and the events that followed it, compelled the suspension of this, as they did of nearly or quite every other college in the Southwest and South, and terminated my labors there. Wishing to engage in similar educational work elsewhere, I asked for testimonials from a few of my friends, including Bishop Smith. He kindly gave the following, with which, as I at that time terminated my labors in the State, I will close this very personal volume, descriptive of my always pleasantly and gratefully remembered life and labors in the Southwest :

LOUISVILLE, KENTUCKY, *September* 19, 1861.

. . . I first knew Dr. Pierson (then Mr. Pierson) when acting as Bible agent in the waste places of Kentucky, and our hearts were strongly drawn toward each other in consequence of our having been "companions in tribulation, and in the kingdom and patience of Jesus Christ "—I having labored and suffered in behalf of the same class of persons as Superintendent of Public Instruction, traveling for the greater part of two years over the roughest portions of Kentucky. To elevate our fellow-creatures so that they can read the Bible for themselves, and then to give to all such a Bible in their own tongues, is a noble work, and great suffering may well be cheerfully endured in the prosecution of it.

His exertions in behalf of the college at Princeton have attracted more of my attention, and elicited my most cordial admiration, beyond anything of the kind in this State for thirty years. The difficulties to be overcome were of no common kind, and the means at his disposal very limited ; the skill with which he met the one, and the wisdom and energy with which he drew forth the other, have rarely been exceeded. And I have it from the lips of the most intelligent persons in the village, during my periodical visits, that no person they ever knew could have awakened equal enthusiasm in so good a cause. For myself, I should have looked upon the task of raising half the sum of twenty thousand dollars in such a village, for such a purpose, as altogether impracticable; and yet Dr. Pierson seemed to succeed with perfect ease.

The teaching he was, of course, obliged to devolve in great measure upon others. But it has come to my knowledge that he was considered the animating spirit of the whole concern. And it is only necessary to converse with him, from time to time, to become impressed with a sense of his literary attainments, fine taste, genial nature, and earnest, unaffected piety.

His loss to the college, should he leave it, will be irreparable, and long will it be before his place will be made good to the general cause of education in the Commonwealth, and in the esteem and affection of

His and your friend, etc.,

B. B. SMITH.

THE END.

www.ingramcontent.com/pod-product-compliance
Lightning Source LLC
Chambersburg PA
CBHW021120270326
41929CB00009B/964